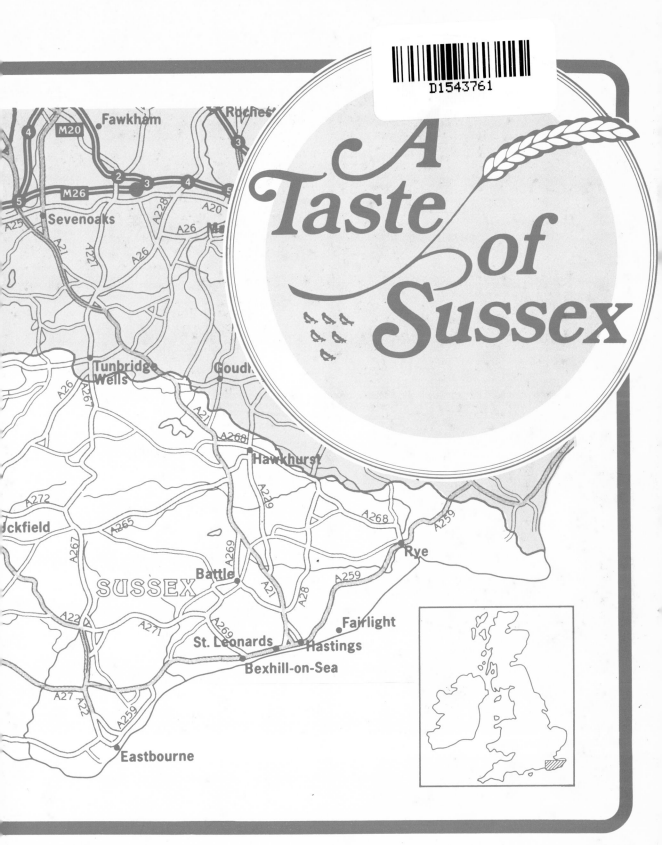

A Taste of Sussex

£4.95

EAST SUSSEX

WEST SUSSEX

Sussex Patron's Messages

"It gives me great pleasure to wish this venture every success and I feel sure it will be a tremendous help towards improving the beauty and quality of products of Sussex".

Lavinia, Duchess of Norfolk
★★★

"I am pleased to add my personal support for "A Taste of Sussex". It is well known that there are many interesting and beautiful things to see in Sussex, but it is now also clear that there are many good and tasty things to eat in Sussex too!"

The Earl of March
★★★

"I am delighted to give my wholehearted support to British Food and Farming in Sussex. We should not take for granted the hard work of all those who play such an important part in growing so much of the food which we buy from our shops, without realising the skills which are necessary to produce this food. This is a most interesting project, and one which is long overdue.

The Earl of Abergavenny
★★★

"My family has been involved in the production of food in Sussex since the twelfth century when the rent was a combination of garlic and arrowheads. Looking back through the records it is clear that the production of food and farming has for the most part been a hard and oft an unrewarding occupation. It is so today and I thus welcome the initiative of British Food and Farming in celebrating the efforts and achievements of those who toil on the land".

Lord Hampden
★★★

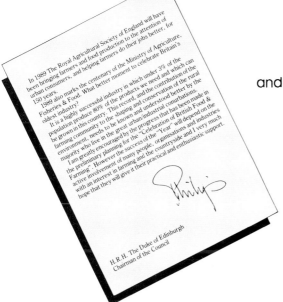

In 1989 The Royal Agricultural Society of England will have been bringing farmers and food production to the attention of urban consumers, and helping farmers do their jobs better, for 150 years.

1989 also marks the centenary of the Ministry of Agriculture, Fisheries & Food. What better moment to celebrate Britain's oldest industry?

It is a highly successful industry in which under 3% of the population produce 80% of the products we need and which can be grown in this country. This record, and the contribution of the farming community to the shaping and understood better by the environment, needs to be known and understood better by the majority who live in the great urban/industrial conurbations.

I am greatly encouraged by the progress that has been made in the preliminary planning for the "Celebration of British Food & Farming". However the success of the "Year" will depend on the active involvement of many people, organisations and industries with an interest in farming and the countryside and I very much hope that they will give it their practical and enthusiastic support.

H.R.H. The Duke of Edinburgh
Chairman of the Council

Foreword

The inspiration to promote the beautiful counties of Sussex with their rolling countryside, coastline, productive farmland and wealth of historic heritage, came as a result of the Celebration Year of British Food and Farming. The incentive to highlight the abundance of fresh, home produced food by way of a Sussex recipe competition produced the theme "A Taste of Sussex" which, in this publication, broadens in significance to include not only the unique taste of fresh produce but places of interest and environmental beauty. Sussex must rate amongst the richest counties in the country in natural beauty, historic legacy and a reputation for fresh food production. Truly an area to visit and explore.

Already "A Taste of Sussex" is destined to live on far beyond the Celebration Year as a result of the enthusiasm of a group of Sussex producers supported by Food From Britain. We, as members of the Sussex Committee of British Food and Farming, are privileged to be able to offer readers a deeper insight into this beautiful area of the country.

Ian Hoyland

Sussex County Co-ordinator
and Principal, West Sussex College of Agriculture

©1989 A Taste of Sussex

Published by A4 Publications Ltd
Pippingford Park Manor, Nutley,
Sussex TN22 3HW, England

Printed in England

ISBN: 0 946197 31 8

1066 Country

In 1066, William the Conqueror fought and won the most famous battle in English history: The Battle of Hastings. The effects of that Norman victory rippled out far and wide and the surrounding countryside developed to meet the needs of its new masters. Castles and towers were built, abbeys, priories and grand country houses. Many remain to tell the tale.

On the spot where "God allowed him to conquer England", William built Battle Abbey. His half-brother Robert built Pevensey Castle and other castles followed in Hastings, Bramber, Lewes and Arundel. Today only the ruins of Hastings Castle cling to the crumbling cliffs and at Bramber only a fragment of tower stands over the River Adur. But Arundel Castle, the home of the Dukes of Norfolk for 700 years, rises magnificently from the meadows of the River Arun, though much of the present building was constructed in Victorian times. William de Warenne built Lewes Castle high above the town and together with his wife Gundrada, said to be William the Conqueror's daughter, founded the great Priory of St. Pancras, later destroyed by Henry VIII.

The magical moated castles at Bodiam (14th century) and Herstmonceux (15th century) were built as protection against the marauding French; in Napoleonic times, Martello Towers were erected along the coast for the same purpose. Several medieval priories remain today: Wilmington, founded by Benedictine monks from Normandy, now houses a collection of agricultural implements; the beautiful moated Michelham Priory, founded by the Augustinians, has musical instruments, tapestries, furniture and toys. Outside there is a Physics Garden and a working watermill.

The twin towns of Rye and Winchelsea have been part of the Confederation of Cinque Ports since 1336 but the sea began to recede from them in the 16th century. Today Rye is a picturesque, walled town with cobbled streets and timbered houses, the local museum in the 13th century Ypres Tower. Winchelsea, said to be the smallest town in England and one of the prettiest, was laid out on a grid pattern in the 13th century to replace Old Winchelsea that was destroyed by the sea.

Stately Homes and Gardens

Walking around the county's stately homes with their elegant treasure-filled rooms, polished stairways and portrait-hung passages, is to take a glimpse into the lives of families whose ownership has spanned the centuries. The Gage family have lived - and still do - at Firle Place near Lewes, for 400 years. Not far away, Glynde Place has belonged to only three families in the same amount of time. Goodwood House in West Sussex has been the seat of the Dukes of Richmond since 1697 and often visited by Royalty for the Goodwood Races. The magnificent Petworth House, home of the Wyndham family, was built in 1688 by the 6th Duke of Somerset, its deer park and pleasure ground added nearly a century later. It has pictures by Van Dyck and Turner, the latter a frequent visitor.

For garden enthusiasts, Sussex is a delight and visitors can take their pick from the great estates with their sweeping lawns and immaculate herbaceous borders, to the tiny cottage gardens

brimming with flowers and vegetables glimpsed over low stone walls and trim white fences.

Some of the country's greatest landscape gardeners have left their mark on these chalk Downland and Wealden clay gardens of Sussex. 'Capability' Brown designed the 150-acre Sheffield Park near Fletching, with its rare trees and shrubs, and lakes that reflect the magnificent rhododendrons growing around them. Humphrey Repton laid out Kidbrooke Park at Forest Row with its pergola, ponds and wild gardens, and Gertrude Jekyll designed the flower beds at Nymans. William Robinson, who introduced the herbaceous border into English gardening, lived at Gravetye, West Hoathly. At Great Dixter the gardens were designed by Sir Edward Lutyens.

Other beautiful gardens to visit include Leonardslee with its lakes and camellia-filled valley and Wakehurst Place with exotic trees and lakes. There's been a garden at West Dean near Singleton since the early 17th century.

Out and About in Sussex

Tramp the South Downs Way from Eastbourne to the Hampshire border (about 86 miles) and you discover the heart of Sussex: wide Downland, deep valleys, winding rivers, small hamlets with their medieval churches and welcoming old pubs. On the cropped grass, wild cowslips and orchids grow, sheep graze and skylarks swoop overhead. You pass Chanctonbury Ring where the Romans built a temple within existing Iron Age ramparts; Ditchling Beacon, at 813 ft. the highest point in East Sussex; and the ancient Long Man of Wilmington carved out of the chalky soil in a time unknown.

The highest point on the south coast is at Beachy Head, just west of Eastbourne where the 534 ft. high white chalk cliffs loom sharply over the sea below. In the 700 acres of the Seven Sisters Country Park where the River Cuckmere ribbons a glittering path through the valley, 45 different kinds of flowers grow wild and terns and waders can be seen on the lagoon. In the east of the county, Rye Harbour has a 585-acre Nature Reserve with shingle beach and wet gravel pits and Hastings Country Park covers 500 acres of unspoilt stretches of coastline. There are the great sandy heathlands of Ashdown Forest where wild

boars once roamed and kings hunted; Friston Forest and the beechwoods of Slindon. On the Commons of Ditchling and Chailey wild flowers grow and wild life flourishes.

The variety of places for family outings in open-air Sussex is endless: wild life parks and nature trails; great reservoirs with their wading birds, ducks and Canada Geese; butterfly centres; an award-winning small zoo; the remains of a Roman Palace. There are steam trains to ride on, working windmills to watch, and farm walks.

Sussex by the Sea

Holidaymakers have been coming to the Sussex coast for over 200 years ever since 1750, when a certain Dr. Russell of Lewes wrote a book on the remedial qualities of Brighton's sea water. In 1783 the Prince Regent put the royal seal of approval on the town by building his palace there.

The county's most westerly resort is Bognor Regis, another town favoured by royalty: Queen Victoria called it her "dear little Bognor" and George V convalesced here and added Regis to its name. Today it's a flourishing family seaside resort with its wide Regency and Victorian seafront, good beach and attractive gardens. Littlehampton, at the mouth of the River Arun, has pleasure crafts in its harbour and red brick Victorian and Edwardian hotels along the front. When just a small fishing village, Worthing was chosen by one of George III's daughters for her convalescence. In Victorian times they built a 900 ft. long pier here and today it's the largest seaside resort in West Sussex and the home of the Bowls Championships. Stately Hove comes next, a town that's inclined to get overlooked in favour of its big neighbouring brother Brighton. But it has a lot going for it: immaculate sea-front lawns, magnificent sports centre, Regency crescents, the County Cricket ground and the internationally acclaimed British Engineerium. Brighton has the magical Royal Pavilion, with its turrets, onion-shaped domes and exotic Chinoiserie; the delightful maze of tiny passages and shops in The Lanes; the recently renovated Palace Pier; and a new Marina, the largest in Europe. The Brighton Festival is held in May each year.

The promenade at Eastbourne has an elegance of its own - three-tiered and three miles long, overlooking golden sands. The town has wide tree-lined streets, beautiful parks, a fine Victorian pier, and a new sport and leisure complex. Young children and senior citizens all approve of Bexhill with its long promenade, safe sandy beaches, well-kept lawns and the famous de la Warr Pavilion that's open every day of the year. In the old town there are antique shops and a church going back to Saxon times.

What is there to see in Hastings? Britain's famous Battle of Hastings in fact took place a few miles inland from here but the remains of William the Conqueror's castle still stand above the town. You can see the unique 243ft long Hastings Embroidery commissioned in 1966 to celebrate the 900th anniversary of the great battle and the Old Town once famous for smuggling still retains its 15th century half-timbered houses, fishing boats and passageways.

County Towns and Country Villages

Chichester is the County Town of West Sussex, and Lewes of East, both ancient places that have kept a sense of history in their narrow streets and medieval buildings.

The Romans built Chichester's walls and called the town Raegnum; the Saxons changed it to Ceastre. Today its 12th century almshouses are still lived in and its four main streets still meet at the 16th century Market Cross. William Blake was tried for treason in the medieval Guildhall and Keats wrote poetry in an 18th century house here. The spire of its magnificent cathedral can be seen for miles around; inside are works by Graham Sutherland, John Piper and Marc Chagall.

Lewes has an 11th century castle, a 14th century Barbican and a 300-year old bowling green that was once a medieval tilting ground. From the top of the castle you can see Offham Hill where Simon de Montfort defeated Henry III and his barons in 1264. Protestant martyrs were burnt at the stake outside the Town Hall in the reign of Mary Tudor and they're remembered each year on November 5 when Lewes celebrates Bonfire Night with spectacular torchlit processions through the town. The very thought of Sussex villages evokes pictures of thatched and timbered cottages clustered round a village green, an ancient church and smugglers' inn. Many have changed little over the years. Some of the most visited include Alfris-

ton with its 'Cathedral of the Downs' and thatched Clergy House built for parish priests in Chaucer's time, the first property to be bought - for £10 in 1891 - by the National Trust; Ditchling, the home of artists and craftsmen for many years; East Dean (in East Sussex) with a 13th century pub and flint cottages; Fletching where Simon de Montfort camped the night before the Battle of Lewes. At the hamlet of Litlington, there's been a Tea House and Pleasure Gardens for over a hundred years. At nearby Lullington, the tiny chapel is only 16ft square. Telscombe is a beautiful medieval village in the Downs on a road that leads to nowhere else. Midhurst, an attractive small town, has a Market Hall built in 1552 and an old Coaching Inn. Steyning's history began in the 8th century with St. Cuthman. Today it still has a thatched Saxon cottage. Findon still has its Great Sheep Fair that has been held there every September since the 13th century. And towering above the River Arun is the town of Arundel with its spectacular castle, winding High Street, 14th century parish church, and 60 acres of wetland with over 1000 wild fowl.

The Arts

The Arts are alive and well and flourishing in Sussex. The Brighton Festival of the Arts and the Chichester Theatre Festival now attract top performers and capacity audiences. Arundel holds its popular Festival in August and Eastbourne has an international Folk Festival in May. Throughout the year there are symphony and pop concerts with international stars; and musical events on a smaller scale in halls around the county.

It was in May 1934 that Glyndebourne, in the heart of the Downs, put on its first opera. Today it's a mecca for opera lovers the world over. The county also has its own opera company: New Sussex Opera.

Both commercial and amateur theatre are immensely popular and there are plenty of places for plays to be performed in: Bexhill-on-Sea has the de la Warr Pavilion: Brighton, the Theatre Royal and the Gardner Arts Centre at Sussex University. There's the Devonshire Park at Eastbourne, and the White Rock Theatre at Hastings.

Craftsmen at Work

The Guild of Sussex Craftsmen was formed nearly 20 years ago to encourage a high standard of work among local craftsmen. Now it has around 50 members producing work of high quality: wood sculpture, ceramics, stoneware, pottery, weaving, thatching, copper, silver and wrought iron work, jewellery, Batik and furniture. The work is sold in shops and galleries and also direct to customers at exhibitions and craft fairs.

Sussex is lucky in that its art galleries put on exhibitions of international importance as well as encouraging less well-known artists.

Literary Sussex

As James Richards, who always used the nom de plume of Jim Cladpole and was fascinated by the Sussex dialect, wrote: "There's summat 'bout Sussex" and the county does seem to have attracted some renowned novelists and poets.

Shelley was born and brought up at Warnham, but only the grave of his son is now to be seen here; in 1819, Keats stayed at Chichester and wrote his St. Agnes Eve poem; Rudyard Kipling lived at Rottingdean and then at Batemans in Burwash; Hilaire Belloc who wrote many poems about Sussex was at Slindon. Richard Jefferies, the naturalist, who gives such a vivid picture of the county in the 1890s, was at Goring-by-Sea; Anthony Trollope at South Harting; and H.G. Wells at Uppark. John Galsworthy spent his holidays at Littlehampton; William Blake composed his famous Jerusalem at Felpham and, something of a contrast, A A Milne's Christopher Robin played 'pooh sticks' in the 100 Acre Wood at Hartfield in Ashdown Forest!

For some years, Lamb House, Rye was home to American novelist Henry James; and Southover

Grange at Lewes, the boyhood home of diarist John Evelyn. W.B. Yeats stayed at Steyning and Virginia and Leonard Woolf's home was at Monk House in Rodmell. Virginia's sister Vanessa lived at Charleston Farm near Lewes, with her husband Clive Bell and artist Duncan Grant, a house much visited by members of the Bloomsbury Group. Other illustrious guests - Oscar Wilde and William Morris - were entertained at Shipley by the poet Wilfrid Scawen Blunt.

Houses open to the public include: Charleston Farm, Batemans, Lamb House, Rye, and Southover Grange.

Perhaps many of these writers had the same thoughts as Hilaire Belloc who wrote:

If ever I became a rich man or if ever I grow to be old,

I will build a house with deep thatch

To shelter me from the cold.

And there shall the Sussex songs be sung

And the story of Sussex be told.

Museum Trail

Sussex is rich in lively museums and they cover an extraordinary variety of subjects: shipwrecks, fishing, archaeology, lifeboats, costumes, toys, fashion, embroidery, geology, marine history, oriental ceramics, coins and medals, military heritage, farming, birds and vintage cars. It is impossible to detail them all but among the more unusual ones are:

The working open-air Amberley Chalk Pits museum near Storrington where you can see the industrial history of the south east; Bramber House of Pipes with 25,000 items from 150 countries; the Martello Tower at Eastbourne showing 19th century defence methods; Horsham Museum with its toys, costumes and folk-life. Hove has the British Engineering, with its hundreds of models and great working 19th century Beam Engine; Lewes, the 15th century Anne of Cleves house with its old domestic furniture and local bric-a-brac. At Pevensey, the Court House Museum has the original Seal of the Borough. Just outside Chichester there's the Mechanical Music and Doll Collection with instruments housed in a converted church.

At the Weald and Downland Open-Air Museum at Singleton, ancient buildings threatened with demolition have been re-erected on this 40-acre site. In the Seven Sisters Country Park's Living World Centre you can see butterflies, ants, spiders, snails, moths and marine life.

Fishing and .....

Over thirty different kinds of fish are brought in off the Sussex coast at Newhaven, Shoreham, Brighton, Eastbourne and Hastings.

The kind of fish varies with the season: Dover Sole, Turbot and Brill in the spring; Skate, Lemon Sole, Turbot, Brill and Squid in summer. In the autumn there's Dover Sole, Cod, Conger Eel, Skate and Whiting. And in the winter Cod, Whiting and Plaice.

Much of it is sold to London and some to France, but there are local fish markets in Shoreham, Brighton and Hastings. In the latter the fish is sold by a Dutch Auction system where bidding starts at the highest price and works down. The number of good fish shops in Sussex can be counted on one hand, according to former local fishmonger Nicholas Roe and co-author (with Lewes restaurateur John Kenward) of "Swish Fish" in which they describe how to shop for and cook locally caught fish. "People should be flexible," he says. "They shouldn't go out looking for a specific kind, but buy whatever's there and looks best. The best, of course, is what's caught locally but you don't know what it's going to be until you get to the shop!"

There's coarse fishing in many of the Sussex rivers, and angling in the reservoirs that support brown and rainbow trout. There's free fishing in Ditchling and Piltdown ponds, and on parts of the Rother and Arun rivers.

......Farming

The first farmers arrived in Sussex some 6000 years ago and the Downs were among the first places to be chosen by Neolithic settlers. Bronze and Iron Age farmers started to clear the great forests and the Romans cultivated wheat and exported it to France. Sheep farming flourished in the 15th and 16th centuries and it was in the mid-19th that John Ellman of Ringmer successfully produced his Southdown breed, out of fashion today because of its fat content.

On the heavy clay of the High Weald in the north and north east of the County, farms were cut out

of the forest. Today most are small family concerns with sheep, cattle and milking cows. On the Kent border, hops are still grown, though the amount is receding. On Pevensey Marshes, there's been a recent change from intensive sheep grazing to arable crops. These are grown too on the Chichester Plain together with large scale vegetables. On the Downs, sheep are still grazed but not in the numbers they once were. Again, much of the land is being ploughed up for crops.

"In recent years there has been a move away from intensive sheep grazing to arable crops particularly wheat," said Ron Harrington of Plumpton Agricultural College. "These produce more money than many forms of livestock. A lot of changes farmers make are directly related to finance charges and rents."

The present economic situation has also caused some to diversify, with farm walks, bed and breakfast accommodation and farmhouse holidays, clay pigeon shooting. One farmer has turned part of his land into a golf course. Others have gone into producing sheep's milk, cheese and yoghurt; keeping angora goats; or running "pick your own" fruit and vegetable businesses.

The traditional annual sheep fair is still held at Findon, and a newer one at Ardingly. Ardingly is home, too, for the South of England Show. There are weekly fat stock markets at Lewes, Heathfield and Hailsham; the latter, mentioned in the Domesday Book, was held in the main street until the turn of the century and is still thriving.

The last ten years or so have seen an increase in the growing of oil seed and forage rape (Britain is the only country to use this word for the crop!); more farmers turning to organic methods; and the setting up of a Farming and Wildlife Advisory Group to advise on how to encourage more wild life on farms.

Food and Drink

Sussex Crumpy, Horsham Hedgehogs, Rye Bay Scallop Pots, Arundel Mullet Pies, Sussex Pond Pudding, Tipsy Sussex Squire, Chanctonbury Carrot Cake, Ashdown Partridge Pudding, Sussex Blanket Pudding, Sussex Heavies........ these are just some of the local traditional dishes that have been handed down the generations and stood the test of time.

And of course, they're cooked with the best local

ingredients: trout from Amberley, cockles and sole from Selsey, honey from Hassocks, smoked fish from Henfield, turkeys from Arlington, mullet from Arundel. Many farmers today are producing free-range eggs, goat and sheep's cheese and yoghurt as well as organically grown fruit and vegetables. Restaurants and pubs all over the county are now serving good food with prices for all pockets. And tea shops are delighting visitors with their home-baked scones and cakes. One of the oldest is Drusillas, its Thatched Barn Restaurant a tea room since 1925.

Sussex is not only a place to find good food, but also good English wine. Vines have been grown here since Roman times but the trade lapsed when in the 12th century it became cheaper to drink French wine. Now the Weald and Downland Vineyards Association has some 50 members with over 200 acres of vineyards. In 1968 Christopher Ann opened The English Wine Centre near Alfriston and in 1975 the first English Wine Festival was held here. This has become an annual event along with the English Wine Fun Run to France on the first weekend of September. Carr Taylor Vineyard, near Hastings, with 21 acres, successfully exports its wine to France; St George's at Waldron supplies both Houses of Parliament and exports to Australia and Japan.

Although not a vineyard, Merrydown at Horam Manor, founded in 1946, was responsible for much of the reawakening of interest in English wine and now produces not only its famous cider, but traditional country wines like elderberry, red currant, gooseberry, wheat and raisin.

In Lewes, Harveys who own many of the county's good pubs, are still brewing their own beer as they have been doing for centuries.

Pubs have existed ever since the Romans put up their inn signs - bushes of vines on long poles - on their newly built roads. In the 17th and 18th centuries they began to grow up along the old coaching routes to the Sussex coast where smugglers would land their contraband in secluded coves and send them on packhorses over ancient tracks.

What's Your Sport?

There are few sports that aren't played in Sussex. But one of the oldest must be the traditional stool-ball, invented over 500 years ago by milkmaids playing with their three-legged milking stools. Not approaching quite such longevity, cricket has been played in the county for 150 years. It was the 3rd Earl of Sheffield who organised the first tours of Australian cricket teams in England, the first matches always being played at Sheffield Park. Today, Hove is home to the County Cricket Club but matches are also held at Eastbourne, Hastings, Horsham and Worthing, and on many a village green.

The first records of racing in Sussex were in 1783 at Brighton, then called Brighthelmstone, with Goodwood coming in some 18 years later. Today, there's racing at Plumpton which, along with Fontwell, presents the two National Hunt courses on the Downs. Lewes once had a popular course but it exists no longer though horses are still trained here. Polo enthusiasts can watch matches at Cowdray Park, Midhurst. Still on horseback, the county has three foxhound packs; The Southdown, the Eridge, and the East Sussex.

There's angling on the four major rivers - Ouse, Cuckmere, Arun and Adur - though a rod licence is required from the Southern Water Authority. Lake fishing can be enjoyed at several reservoirs; you can take deep sea trips from Littlehampton and Brighton; and fish from resort piers.

For boating enthusiasts, there are moorings at marinas in Brighton, (which has a large racing section), Newhaven, Shoreham Harbour and on the River Arun at Littlehampton and Ford. Small boats are available for hire at Arundel and Houghton and in the summer months there's a river cruise from Littlehampton to Arundel. You can sail at many of the reservoirs including Weir Wood, Bewl Water and Ardingly, and if you don't know how to do so, you can learn on the Hove Lagoon. The Southern Leisure Centre near Chichester offers water ski-ing and boating.

Tennis, bowls and croquet players, golfers and horse riders are all well catered for and for walkers there are some excellent circular routes as well as the marvellous 86-mile long South Downs Way that stretches from Eastbourne in the East to Butser just over the Hampshire border.

Starters, Snacks and Suppers

Recipes in this section use a wide variety of high quality vegetables readily available in Sussex. Indeed, vegetarians will welcome the inclusion of a number of dishes that they too can enjoy. Some of the recipes utilise Sussex table wine from the many vineyards established on the south facing slopes of the Downs. An unusual feature perhaps, is recipes using yoghurt and a variety of cheeses made from sheep's milk, an interesting addition to the wide range of Sussex produce.

Vegetarian Churdles

Serves 6

200g (8 oz)	plain wholemeal flour	
50g (2oz)	white vegetable fat	
50g (2oz)	margarine	shortcrust pastry
pinch	salt	
	water	
50g (2oz)	potato - finely diced	
50g (2oz)	carrot - finely diced	
50g (2oz)	mushrooms - chopped	
50g (2oz)	peas	
1	medium onion - chopped	
1 tablesp	cooking oil	
1 hpd tablesp	chopped parsley	
2 teasp	brown breadcrumbs	
2 teasp	cheese - finely grated	

1. Make shortcrust pastry and leave to rest.
2. Sweat all the vegetables in the cooking oil for about 5 minutes and leave to cool; add parsley.
3. Roll out the pastry and cut into 12 x 12cm (4in) rounds.
4. Cut a cross in the centre of 6 of the circles; these form the tops.
5. Place the vegetable mixture on the 6 uncut circles, dampen the edges and place the cut circles on top, seal the edges.
6. Open the cut tops and add breadcrumbs and cheese.
7. Bake in a moderately hot oven (Gas No. 5, 190 degrees C, 375F) for 30 minutes.

Mrs Audrey P Broad, Southwater

Smoked Salmon in Orbit

Serves 4

4 slices	smoked salmon
1	lemon - juice
4 leaves	crisp lettuce
12	medium to large strawberries
black pepper freshly milled	
1 tablesp	mayonnaise
Half teasp	curry paste
2 teasp	dill - finely chopped
1 tablesp	whipped cream
4 fronds	dill for garnish

1. Lay smoked salmon slices on a sheet of greaseproof paper and brush with lemon juice.
2. Place a lettuce leaf on each side, trimmed to the size of the salmon.
3. Halve strawberries and sprinkle with pepper, place 5 halves across each leaf.
4. Mix the mayonnaise with curry paste and add chopped dill, fold in cream. Spoon the mixture across the strawberry halves.
5. Roll each salmon slice and filling and brush with lemon juice.
6. Chill, serve garnished with remaining strawberry halves and dill.

Mrs M R Finnerty, Sayers Common

Halloumi Cheese Oregano Tomatoes

1 or 2	small onions - sliced
1/2	green pepper - sliced
1 tablesp	oil
1 clove	garlic-crushed
400g (1 lb)	tomatoes-skinned and chopped (or tinned)
2 teasps	oregano
1 teasp	brown sugar
2 teasps	Worcestershire sauce (or Tabasco)
50g (2oz)	cashew nuts
black pepper	
blended cornflour to thicken	
200g(8oz)	Sussex High Weald Halloumi Cheese

1. Fry the onions, green pepper and garlic in oil in a deep frying pan until golden and tender.
2. Add tomatoes, oregano, sugar, sauce, nuts and pepper, simmer on a low heat.
3. Thicken with blended cornflour, stirring all the time.
4. Rinse the Halloumi cheese in cold water to wash off the brine
5. Cut the cheese into 1cm (1/2") cubes and dry fry in a non stick pan until golden brown on one or two of the cube surfaces.
6. Mix the cooked cheese with the tomato mixture and serve on a bed of rice.

Katherine Mowbray, Duddleswell

Filled Buckwheat Crepes

Serves 8-10

1	large egg	⎫
100ml (3 1/2 fl oz)	milk	⎬ crepes
65g (2 1/2 oz)	buckwheat flour	⎭
65g (2 1/2 oz)	cooked spinach	
200ml (7 1/2 fl oz)	vegetable stock	
1 clove	garlic - crushed	
1 pinch	mixed spice	
1 pinch	ginger	
3	large eggs	
2 tablesp	cream	
1 teasp	soy sauce	
25 g (1 oz)	butter	
125g (5 oz)	pearl barley	

1. Liquidise the crepe ingredients and season to taste.
2. Fry as 6 crepes in a 15cm (6 in) pan, use these to line a greased 1 litre (2 pt) terrine dish allowing an overlap at the sides.
3. Liquidise the spinach, stock, garlic, spices, eggs, cream and soy sauce.
4. Melt the butter and glaze the barley, add to the other ingredients.
5. Pour the mixture into the lined dish, cover with the overlapping crepes.
6. Cover with the lid or foil and bake in a cool oven (Gas No. 2, 150 degrees C, 300 F) for 40-60 minutes, until set.
7. Chill for 12 hours before serving.

Nigel Catterall, Northiam

Poultry Parcels

Serves 8

Shortcrust pastry		
400g (1 lb)	plain flour	
100g (4 oz)	margarine	shortcrust pastry
100g (4 oz)	lard	
	Cold water	
100g (4 oz)	dried prunes - soaked for 4 hours	
1	large onion - finely chopped	
100g (4 oz)	cooking apple - coarsely grated	
	fresh white breadcrumbs	
	lemon - grated rind	
	salt and pepper	
1	egg - beaten	
400g (1 lb)	cooked chicken - minced	

1. Make the shortcrust pastry, leave to rest while preparing the filling.
2. Drain the prunes, discard the stones and chop finely.
3. Mix the prunes, onion, apple, breadcrumbs, lemon rind, seasoning and egg in a large bowl and add minced chicken; mix well.
4. Roll out pastry and cut into 8 x 20cm (8 in) circles using a pan lid.
5. Pile the prune and chicken mixture on the pastry circles, damp edges and fold each over; seal edges.
6. Glaze with milk or egg and bake in a moderately hot oven (Gas No. 6, 200C 400F) for 15 minutes then reduce to a moderate oven (Gas No. 4, 180 degrees C, 350F) for a further 30 minutes.

Mrs Avril Joy Banting, Findon Valley

Cashew Nut and Mushroom Loaf

Serves 4

1 tablesp	oil
2	shallots - chopped
3 cloves	garlic - crushed
200g (8oz)	cashew nuts
1	egg - beaten
1 teasp	chopped chives
1 teasp	chopped thyme
3	parsnips
100ml (4fl oz)	vegetable stock
1 teasp	yeast extract
	salt and pepper
25g (1oz)	butter
200g (8oz)	button mushrooms - finely sliced

1. Heat oil in a saucepan and saute shallots and garlic until soft.
2. Liquidise or grind the nuts to look like coarse breadcrumbs.
3. Place nuts in a bowl and add egg, herbs and sauted shallot.
4. Peel and chop the parsnips, boil until soft, mash well and add to nut mixture.
5. Heat the vegetable stock and dissolve the yeast extract in it, add to nut mixture and mix all together thoroughly.
6. Heat butter and fry mushrooms until soft.
7. Grease and line a 1 kilo (2lb) loaf tin. Press in half the nut mixture, spread a layer of mushrooms, cover with remaining mixture.
8. Wrap the loaf tin in foil and bake in a moderate oven (Gas No. 4, 180 degrees C, 350F) for 1 1/4 hours.
9. Remove from oven and allow to stand for 10 minutes before turning out.
10. Serve hot or cold.

Lucy Ann, Alfriston

Harvest Crumble

Serves 4-6

1 tablesp	sunflower oil
1 clove	garlic - crushed
1	large onion - chopped
1 head	celery - chopped
100g (4oz)	mushrooms - sliced
100g (4oz)	nuts - chopped
50g (2oz)	butter - melted
1 small loaf	wholemeal or granary bread - crumbed
150g (6oz)	mature Cheddar cheese - grated
25g (1oz)	rolled oats
1 teasp	wholegrain mustard
salt and pepper	
6	large tomatoes
300ml (1/2 pt)	water
2 teasp	tomato puree
2 teasp	yeast extract

1. Heat oil in pan and sweat vegetables until soft, stir in nuts.
2. Pour melted butter into breadcrumbs and add cheese, oats, mustard and seasoning and mix well.
3. In an ovenproof dish put the vegetables and nut mixture, half the crumb mixture, the sliced tomatoes.
4. Heat the water and dissolve the tomato puree and yeast extract, pour over tomatoes.
5. Top with the remaining crumb mixture.
6. Bake in a moderately hot oven (Gas No. 5, 190 degrees C, 375F) for 30 minutes.

Jackie Wood, Bexhill-on-Sea

Horsham Hedgehogs

See photograph page 15

Serves 4

400g (1 lb)	sausagemeat
1	large onion - finely chopped
1 teasp	mixed herbs
	salt and pepper
1	egg - beaten
100g (4 oz)	brown breadcrumbs - coarse

1. Mix sausagemeat, onion, herbs and seasoning.
2. Form balls of mixture into hedgehog shapes, dip in beaten egg and roll in breadcrumbs.
3. Place hedgehogs on a baking tray and cook in a moderate oven (Gas No. 4, 180C, 350F) for 25 minutes until crumb 'spines' are crisp.

Mrs N S Bryant, Llanedeyrn

Putlands Cheese Souffle

Serves 2

3	fresh farm eggs
2/3 cup	Sussex High Weald Dairy Sheep Ricotta cheese
1 1/2 cups	Sussex High Weald Dairy Sheep mature cheese - grated
salt and pepper	

1. Add eggs to Ricotta cheese and beat slightly.
2. Add 3/4 cup grated cheese and seasoning and beat until well mixed.
3. Pour into a 1 litre (2 pt) well greased souffle dish and sprinkle 3/4 cup grated cheese on top.
4. Bake in a hot oven (gas No. 8, 230 degrees C, 450F) for about 25 minutes.

Mrs G St J Hardy, Duddleswell

Fun, Animals and Wine

Drusillas means different things depending on how old you are.

For the oldest, it means remembering a small Sussex farm developing into a refreshment stop to sustain the tourists in the earliest days of motoring. As roadhouses sprung up, competition became keen and Drusillas sought to offer more attractions for the customer. By the '30s it was a place with a small zoo, a railway which ran to the river Cuckmere half a mile away and a place where boats and punts were hired out. Apart from lunches and Sussex teas, dances were held nightly. Evening dress was essential and egg and bacon suppers were included in the price of 2/6d (12.5p) a head; guests brought their own drinks.

During the Second World War, Captain Douglas Ann, who started Drusillas in 1925, was called up. His wife Elizabeth continued to run the tea place but all other attractions closed down. The zoo animals dispersed and the steam train was shot up by troops for target practice.

After the War, Drusillas started to grow rapidly into the famous leisure attraction it is today, a place which draws thousands of children and adults every year.

One son, Michael Ann, developed the Zoo Park as a Rare Breeds Survival Centre for the old domestic type of cattle and sheep which are vital to the maintenance of the productive cross breeds of today. He also concentrated on developing the zoo to a level where it became of educational interest to the Sussex and Surrey Educational Authorities. The facilities offered in the inclusive ticket for schools are the zoo tour, with printed and pictorial worksheets for different age groups, the great playground with its specially developed climbing frames, fire engine, tractors, landrover and the ever popular train.

The English Wine Centre, which is well known for its stock of both English and world wines, is situated a few yards down the road from Drusillas. In September 1975 the first Festival of English Wine was held attracting enthusiasts and winemakers from all over Britain as well as Europe. Wine enthusiast Christopher Ann recorded talks for the BBC overseas service and even for Thai radio. The Wine Festival continues to take place annually. An ever increasing number of daily visitors to the English Wine Centre enjoy buying wine in the relaxed atmosphere and wine tours and tastings never cease to be popular.

Drusillas Park at Alfriston East Sussex, is one of the most fascinating leisure attractions in the county. The 400,000 children and adults who visit each year obviously think so too!.

Drusillas Park, Alfriston, East Sussex, BN26 5QS. Tel (0323) 870234 (Functions and Wine Tel (0323) 870164)

Cheese Curry

Serves 4

25g (1 oz)	butter or margarine
1	onion - chopped
2	eating apples - cored and diced
50g (2 oz)	wholemeal flour
3-4 teasp	curry powder
600ml (1 pt)	chicken stock
4 level tablesp	sweet pickle
50g (2 oz)	sultanas
200g (8 oz)	cheese - diced
	seasoning to taste

1. Melt the butter and saute the onion, add the apples and cook for 1 minute, stir in flour and curry powder.
2. Blend in the stock, and the rest of the ingredients except the cheese and cook for a few minutes.
3. Add cheese and stir until melted, serve immediately with rice.

Mrs V M King, Bexhill-on-Sea

Sussex Crumpy

Serves 4

2 rashers	bacon
1	onion - chopped
2	tomatoes - sliced
50g (2oz)	mushrooms - sliced
4	eggs
4 tablesp	cream
50g (2oz)	cheddar cheese - grated
	pepper

1. Grease a deep pie dish or souffle dish.
2. Snip the bacon into small pieces and fry, add onion and saute.
3. Put these in dish and add tomatoes and mushrooms.
4. Beat eggs and cream together, add cheese and pepper, pour over ingredients in dish.
5. Cook in a moderate oven (Gas No. 4, 180 degrees C, 350F) for 35 minutes.

Mrs Prunella Guthrie, Amberley

Holmes Hill Delight

Serves 3

3	red skinned eating apples
1	lemon - juice
185g (7 1/2 oz)	tuna
1/2	green pepper - chopped
1/2	red pepper - chopped
1/2 bunch	radishes - diced
100 g (4 oz)	goat's cheese (soft)
	salt and pepper

1. Core and scoop out the apples, leaving 8mm (1/4") layer, brush with lemon juice.
2. Chop the removed apple and to it add the flaked tuna, peppers, radishes and goats cheese, season and mix well.
3. Pile mixture into the apple shells, chill and serve on a bed of lettuce with the remaining mixture served separately.

Melanie Harris, Priory School, Lewes

Holmes Hill Delight

Horsham Hedgehog

900 Years of History

A Castle has overlooked the town of Arundel and the River Arun for nearly a thousand years. It all started in 1067 when Roger de Montomery was created Earl of Arundel by William the Conqueror.

The first fortification at Arundel was made of timber. This was soon replaced by the stone

Keep which stands proudly at the centre of the Castle today. Over the centuries, many Dukes have added, modified, and extended.

During the Civil War, Arundel Castle was besieged and sacked by Parliamentary forces under the command of Sir William Waller. It was Waller who mounted his guns on top of the tower of the parish church to enable his men to fire down inside the walls. As a result, the Castle remained in ruins till the 18th Century.

The fourteenth Duke, Henry Grenville, started to reconstruct the Castle but died before the work was completed. The Castle was finally restored by his son Henry, the fifteenth Duke.

Arundel Castle is one of the most fascinating places to visit in West Sussex. The Library, the Baron's Hall and the Fitzalan Chapel are among the most magnificent rooms. All contain a wealth of treasures - furniture from the 16th Century, paintings by Mytens, Van Dyke, Gainsborough, Reynolds and other great painters, tapestries, clocks - even the gilt state bed made for Queen Victoria's visit in 1846.

The Castle and grounds are open to visitors from 24 March to the last Friday in October - Sundays to Fridays from 1-5 pm and from 12 Noon throughout June, July, August and on all Bank Holidays. The last admission on any day is 4pm. The Castle does not open on Saturdays.

Enjoy 900 years of history at Arundel Castle, Arundel, West Sussex. Tel: (0903) 883136.

Vegetable Curry

Serves 4-6
(Using 11 Sussex grown vegetables bought from a local farm shop!)

2 tablesp	sunflower oil
1	small onion - chopped
2	carrots - diced
100g (4oz)	mushrooms - chopped
1/4	green pepper - chopped
1	leek - sliced
2 sticks	celery - sliced
1	large potato - diced
florets	cauliflower
1	small swede - diced
1	turnip - chopped
50g (2oz)	green beans
1	dessert apple - diced
2 1/2 teasp	curry paste
25g (1oz)	plain flour
150ml (1/4 pt)	stock
1 teasp	lemon juice
1	bay leaf
2 tablesp	sultanas
125g (5oz)	natural yoghurt
200g (8oz)	long grain brown rice

1. Heat the oil in a large pan and saute the vegetables and fruit.
2. Stir in the curry paste and flour and cook for 3 minutes.
3. Add the stock and bring to the boil, add the lemon juice, bay leaf and sultanas and finally gently pour in the yoghurt.
4. Simmer for 30 to 35 minutes and serve with boiled brown rice.

Sally Entecott, Robertsbridge School

Spiced Spinach and Halloumi Cheese

Serves 4-6

500g (1 lb)	spinach - fresh (or frozen)
1/2	red pepper
2	small onions
1	clove garlic
25 g (1 oz)	fat or oil for frying
200g (8 oz)	rice
200g (8 oz)	Sussex High Weald Halloumi Cheese

1. Wash spinach, remove stems and chop roughly. Boil in a little salted water until tender.
2. Drain the spinach, retaining the cooking water in which to boil the rice.
3. Peel and chop onions, garlic and pepper.
4. Melt the fat and fry the onion, pepper and garlic until golden and tender.
5. Add the drained spinach and simmer until dry; season with black pepper.
6. Boil the rice, using the spinach water.
7. Rinse the Halloumi cheese to remove the brine in which it is preserved, cut it into 1 cm (1/2") cubes.
8. Fry the cheese cubes in a dry non-stick frying pan until golden brown on one or two of the surfaces. Add the fried cheese to the spinach mixture.
9. Place the cooked rice around an ovenproof dish and pile the spiced spinach and Halloumi cheese in the centre. Serve immediately.

Katherine Mowbray, Duddleswell

Yoghurt and Cucumber Salad

50g (2 oz)	dessicated coconut
2 tablesp	hot water/milk
12g (1/2 oz)	butter
1 teasp	black mustard seed
300ml (1/2 pt)	sheeps milk yoghurt
1	large cucumber - peeled and sliced
1/4	green pepper - chopped finely
1 teasp	salt

1. Soak coconut in hot water/milk for 30 minutes.
2. Heat butter in a small pan and fry mustard seeds, with the lid on, until they pop.
3. Add cooked mustard seeds and butter to yoghurt and combine with cucumber, pepper and soaked coconut.
4. Add salt, chill and serve cold.

Katherine Mowbray, Duddleswell

South Downs Terrine

Serves 8

300g (12 oz)	firm belly pork - derinded and minced finely
150g (6 oz)	lean green bacon - minced coarsely
1 glass	white wine (optional)
juniper berries - crushed	
pepper corns - crushed	
25g (1 oz)	hazel kernels

1. Mix minced pork and bacon with wine and season with crushed juniper berries and peppercorns.
2. Stir in the hazel kernels and pack the mixture into a small loaf tin, cover with the pork rind.
3. Cover with foil and place in a roasting tin of water.
4. Cook in a moderate oven (Gas No. 4, 180 degrees C, 350F) for about 1 hour.
5. Allow to cool and place in the refrigerator overnight.

Elizabeth Clarke, Birdham

Celery Crunch

Serves 4

4	celery hearts
chicken stock	
salt and pepper	
1 dab	butter
4	slices ham
450ml (3/4 pt)	cheese sauce
50g (2 oz)	cheese grated
50g (2 oz)	brown breadcrumbs
cornflakes or plain crisps - crushed	

1. Braise celery in chicken stock with seasoning and butter.
2. Wrap each celery heart in a slice of ham and place in an ovenproof dish.
3. Cover with a cheese sauce and top with a mixture of cheese, breadcrumbs and either crushed crisps or cornflakes.
4. Place in a moderate oven (Gas No. 4, 180 degrees C, 350F) for 30 minutes or until the top is crisp.

Mrs M Bushby, Sidlesham

A Taste of Cheese

Sussex is not generally regarded as a cheese-making county. Now all that is changing , with the advent of milk quotas and increasing public awareness of wholesome, natural, additive-free foods.

Castle Hill Farm is one place where you can see how cheese is made. Cheesemaking experiments began on the kitchen stove using a plastic drainpipe as a mould. In 1986, the farm started making cheese in a small way in a converted cowshed. As the demand grew, more equipment was made and antique presses of various types were brought from around the country. An old Victorian dairy was converted into a cheese store and Sussex Farmhouse Cheese was sold at local shows.

As the name spread, visitors began to come in increasing numbers. Parties of school children and other groups come in the mornings during the week to see round the farm. Most are surprised how labour intensive cheesemaking is.

Milk is used from Friesian cows, together with a starter culture, to get the right bacteria developing in the milk. The rennet is non-animal in origin and the only other ingredient is salt. Then the cheese is matured on shelves, to give it a traditional flavour.

Today, the farm makes over 800lbs a week.

Visit, smell and taste for yourselves at Castle Hill Farm, Rotherfield, East Sussex.
Tel:(089 285) 2207

A Taste for Cricket

It is said that the game of cricket was invented by shepherds guarding their flocks on the South Downs. Cricket has certainly been played in Sussex for 150 years and for the majority of these the home of Sussex cricket has been at Hove.

Sussex may never have won the County Championship, but they have won the Gillette Cup three times and the NatWest Trophy once as well as giving many famous names to the game - from Gilligan to Greig and Dexter to Duleep Sinhji. In fact, Ted Dexter captained the side when they won the first two Gillette Cups and were commonly considered the best one-day cricket team in the UK.

Further back in history, C Aubrey Smith, the Hollywood actor, was captain of the

Sussex team at the turn of the century and went on to start the first Hollywood Cricket Team.

The Sussex Cricket Club headquarters has been operating for 120 years and is in desperate need of improvement.

Fund-raising activities are underway to raise money to improve the players' dressing rooms and the members' stand as well as assisting in the provision of indoor cricket nets.

As recently as 1986, Sussex won a major trophy but, since then, the team has been somewhat in the doldrums. What could be better for them, in this period of major fund-raising than to win a major trophy in the near future?

Birch's Pier

The famous West Pier at Brighton was built by Eugenius Birch in 1866. Although Birch built 14 others, this one is considered to be his crowning achievement. The Pier is recognised as a superb example of Victorian maritime engineering and architecture and a structure of national and historic importance. In November 1982, it was granted Grade 1 listed status, the only Pier in Britain so to be honoured.

The Pier was opened in October 1866. The Pavilion was built in 1893, landing stages for paddle steamers added in 1896 and the famous Concert Hall added in 1916. Activities included plays, revues, opera, ballet and symphony concerts.

Between the wars, admission was 2 shillings (10p) for a matinee including teas and a visit to the comic opera was 4 pence (less than 2p). Admission to the Pier with a pram was 2 pence but three times as much for a bath chair.

Sadly, the Pier was closed to the public in 1975 due to deterioration of the structure from time, the sea and the elements.

The Brighton West Pier Trust is a registered Charitable Organisation working to put that right, to restore the Pier to its former glory and once again to open it to the public. The West Pier represents a unique part of Brighton's seafront and the nation's heritage which, once lost, can never be replaced.

The Trust has received generous grants from English Heritage, the National Heritage Memorial Fund and Brighton Borough Council. Some renovation work was completed in 1987 and the landward end of the Pier reopened to the public for the first time in 12 years. Despite further damage from the hurricane in October 1987, plans for restoration are moving again. The aim is to ensure that renovation will be in sympathy with the Pier's historic and Grade 1 status.

The West Pier is recovering but it needs the support of the public. Anyone can help make the West Pier live again by making a donation or by becoming a member of the Trust for just £10. **For more information, contact the West Pier Trust, North West House, West Street, Brighton BN1 1RR. Tel: (0273) 21499.**

Grannie Skitt's Bacon Pudding

Serves 6

200g (8 oz)	Self-raising flour	
100g (4 oz)	shredded suet	suet crust pastry
pinch	salt	
	water to mix	

200g (8 oz)	smoked bacon or ham, chopped
1	large onion, chopped
1	large cooking apple, peeled and chopped
pinch	sage
salt and pepper	

1. Mix flour, suet and salt with sufficient water to form a firm dough.
2. Roll out to an oblong shape about 1/2 a cm (1/4 inch) thick.
3. Spread with the filling mixture of bacon, onion and apple, sprinkle with sage and season.
4. Roll up and tie in a floured cloth, boil for 2 hours.

Mrs Anne Skitt, Westham

Fish Dishes

The rich harvest from the sea off the Sussex coast inspired many competitors to offer dishes using fish. Recipes have been selected using scallops, prawns, mackerel, herring, coding, plaice, sole and mullet which are but a few of the fish brought in by the fishermen of Sussex. There are now trout farms in many parts of the county so some tasty recipes for trout are included.

Hastings Herrings

Serves 4

4	herrings - filleted
	salt and pepper
1	onion - chopped
450ml (3/4 pt)	dry cider
	peppercorns
1cm (1/2 in)	root ginger
1	bay leaf.

1. Halve herrings, season and roll with skin inwards from tail end.
2. Place in ovenproof dish, add other ingredients.
3. Bake in a cool oven (Gas No. 2 150 degrees C, 300F) for 1 hour.
4. Leave to cool for 30 minutes.
5. Arrange herrings in serving dish and pour over strained cooking liquid
6. Cover and chill before serving.

Jill Hazel, Seaford

Arundel Mullet Pies

Serves 4

250g (10oz)	Arundel mullet fillets
125ml (1/4pt)	English white wine
125ml (1/4pt)	cider vinegar
	Bouquet garni of fresh herbs:
	lemon balm, fennel and summer savoury
	salt and peppercorns
300g (12oz)	shortcrust pastry
25g (1oz)	sliced mushrooms
2	chopped shallots
12g (1/2oz)	butter
125ml (1/4pt)	coating white sauce made with fish liquor
	eggwash

1. Prepare a court bouillon with wine, cider and bouquet garni and sufficient water to cover the fish, bring to the boil
2. Poach the mullet fillets for 10 mins and allow to cool in liquor.
3. Make the pastry and allow to rest in a cool place.
4. Sweat the mushrooms and shallots in the butter until soft.
5. Prepare sauce and add mushroom mixture and flaked fish; season.
6. Divide the pastry into 4 and roll out each piece to about 150mm x 100mm (7in x 4in). Fold in half and using template cut out to the shape of a fish.
7. Place on some filling, dampen edges with eggwash, fold together and shape as a fish. Mark on scales and add pastry fins.
8. Glaze and bake for 20 mins in a moderately hot oven, Gas No 5, 190C, 375F.
9. Garnish with lemon and watercress and bunches of white grapes.

Valerie Rankin, Lyminster

Rye Bay Scallop Pots

Serves 2

2	small sheets of pre-rolled frozen puff pastry
1	egg - beaten
12g (1/2 oz)	butter
1	shallot - finely chopped
2	rashers smoked back bacon - chopped
4	Rye Bay scallops - cleaned and sliced into 4
100ml (3 fl oz)	dry white wine
dash	lemon juice
100ml (3 fl oz)	double cream
salt and freshly milled black pepper	
1 tablesp	chopped parsley

1. Preheat oven to Gas no. 8, 230 degrees C, 450F.
2. Cut the pastry squares in half diagonally to form 4 triangles. On 2 of the triangles cut/mark an inner triangle 1cm (1/2 in) from the edge. Score the inner triangle with criss cross cuts - this will form the lid.
3. Brush the unmarked triangles with beaten egg and place the others on top. Knock up the edges.
4. Glaze with beaten egg and bake 10-15 minutes until well risen and golden. Remove the inner triangles and reserve as the lids.
5. Melt the butter in a frying pan and add the chopped shallot and bacon, fry gently until beginning to brown.
6. Add the scallops and fry them lightly. Add the wine and lemon juice and poach the scallops for a minute or until lightly cooked.
7. Remove the scallops, bacon and shallot from the pan, using a slotted spoon.
8. Reduce the liquor in the pan to 1/4, add the cream and stir in. Bring almost to the boil.
9. Remove the pan from the heat and add the scallops, bacon and shallots. Pour onto the prepared pastry pots, top with the lids and serve with a wedge of fresh lemon.

Sarah J Card, A Sussex Fisherman's Wife, Newhaven

Arundel Mullet Pie

Honey and Lemon Mousse (see page 48)

Local Fish Supper

Serves 4

400g (1 lb)	locally caught fish, cooked and flaked
2	tomatoes
1	onion - finely chopped
	seasoning
25g (1 oz)	margarine
25g (1 oz)	flour
300ml (1/2 pt)	milk
100g (4 oz)	cheese - grated
50g (2 oz)	wholemeal breadcrumbs

1. Place the flaked fish in an ovenproof dish, cover with sliced tomato and chopped onion, season to taste.
2. Make a cheese sauce by the roux method and pour over the fish.
3. Sprinkle with breadcrumbs and bake at Gas No. 5, 190 degrees C, 325F for 30 minutes.

Claire Osborn, Worthing

Crispy Cod with Pancakes

Serves 4

400g (1 lb)	smoked cod
150ml (1/4 pt)	milk
	black pepper
4	wholemeal pancakes
450ml (3/4 pt)	pouring white sauce
100g (4 oz)	Gruyere cheese - grated
2 packets	ready salted crisps - crushed

1. Place the cod and milk in a shallow pan and poach the fish for approximately 10 minutes, or until the fish flakes.
2. Allow the fish to cook then blend to a puree with a little black pepper.
3. Arrange the fish puree, pancakes and sauce in layers in a deep dish.
4. Combine the cheese and crisps and sprinkle over the top, bake in a moderate oven (Gas No. 4, 180 degrees C, 250F) for 20 minutes.

Miss Linda Henty, Eastbourne

Marinaded Trout

1	trout (as large as possible)
1 hpd teasp	salt
1 rnd teasp	sugar
1 teasp	ground black pepper
1 tablesp	brandy
	dillweed

1. Split trout and remove the bones.
2. Mix the marinade, using the other ingredients except the dillweed
3. Rub the marinade into both sides of the fish, sprinkle with dillweed
4. Cover with foil and press for 12 hours to 14 days in a refrigerator.

Mrs G St J Hardy, Duddleswell

45,000 Objects

The Antiques Roadshow has made everyone wary of throwing almost anything away. Everyone hopes to find a treasure in the attic, and just about everyone knows that Sotheby's are world experts on the subject of antiques and fine art.

But not everyone knows that Summers Place in Billingshurst is the largest auction saleroom in Great Britain outside London selling over 45,000 objects every year.

Summers Place is set in the beautiful Sussex countryside. Here over 70 staff are employed and you will find the same sort of extensive range of services you would expect to find in Sotheby's headquarters in London or New York.

Whether selling, buying, browsing or just curious to find out how much the family heirloom is worth, Summers Place is well worth

visiting - and a perfect place for a day out. There are always interesting things to see both inside the impressive late Victorian mansion and within the 40 acres of grounds. There is plenty to see, ample room to park and a restaurant to enjoy.

Verbal valuations and advice on any item are available free to anyone, without any obligation to place the item for sale. So if you have something that you think might be of interest, take it along for an opinion - it costs nothing to ask.

At Summers Place, Sotheby's have five salerooms for auctions of furniture, silver, ceramics and paintings as well as more unusual items such as clocks, wine, horse-drawn vehicles, garden statues and architectural pieces. Specialised and general sales are held throughout the year, attracting buyers and sellers from around the world - open to anyone, quite free of charge.

Summers Place is open Monday to Friday from 9.30 am to 4.30 pm and Saturday from 9.30 am to 12.30 pm. To avoid disappointment, you can telephone beforehand to ensure the expert you wish to consult is available.

Enjoy an unusual (perhaps a very profitable) visit to Sotheby's at Summers Place, Billingshurst, West Sussex RH14 9AD. Tel: (040381) 3933).

Alfred Duke 'Gone to Earth' oil on canvas signed, 17.5 by 23.25ins. Sold at Sotheby's Sussex for £3,410

A Glass apart

The origins of cider are lost in the mists of time. But one well documented fact concerns 400 gallons of cider which two enthusiastic amateur winemakers, Ian Howie and Jack Ward, made in the garage of Jack's house in 1946. From those gallons, together with a similar quantity of Red Currant wine from locally grown fruit, flowed the beginnings of famous drinks. Deep in the heart of the Sussex Weald, the two men decided to call their company, and its products, Merrydown after the name on the front gate!.

In less than a year, the garage proved too small for the enterprise. So the partners acquired the ruins of a once stately home called

Horam Manor. Gradually, over the years, a modern cider mill and winery grew up around the foundations of the old Manor. Today, bottling lines, vats, warehouses and offices cover seven acres.

In addition to cider, Merrydown has continued the tradition of producing real country wines. Redcurrant, Elderberry and Damson are a range of red wines proving that not only can the grape be fermented but that it will produce an interesting and satisfactory drink. Sparkling Strawberry. Peach and Elderflower, under the '1066' label, have been added to the range. Also produced at Horam are Martlet Cider Vinegar and Honegar, popular for more than 30 years among the health conscious. More recently, the range has been extended to include speciality vinegars Tarragon, Dill, Garlic, Raspberry, Red and White Wine to add interest to a variety of foods.

Bigger today than they ever dreamt possible, the same sound basic principles of Ian Howie and Jack Ward still apply. Only the finest ingredients are used and, whenever possible, bought locally. The use of artificial flavouring, colouring and sweetenings is avoided. Care, skill and true craftsmanship go towards producing the finest possible range of ciders, wines and vinegars.

Merrydown has grown to become the fourth largest cider producer in the UK and one of the leaders of real English Country Wines. Today it proudly upholds a tradition of cider and wine making in Sussex which has survived for almost a 1000 years.

Come and see cider being made - April to October. Tel (04353) 2401.

Stuffed Mackerel

Serves 2

2	large fresh mackerel
50g (2 oz)	butter
1	small onion - finely chopped
50g (2 oz)	mushrooms - finely chopped
1	small Bramley apple - cored
1 glass	white wine
1 slice	wholemeal bread - crumbed
pinch	salt
grind	black pepper
1/4 teasp	dried thyme
sprigs	parsley for garnish

1. Remove heads from mackerel, gut and descale. Wash and set aside.
2. Melt 25g (1 oz) butter and saute onion and mushrooms.
3. Cut 2 thick rings from the middle of the apple and poach them for 2-3 minutes in white wine.
4. Chop the remaining apple and add it to the onion and mushroom mixture, cook until the apple softens.
5. Remove pan from heat and add breadcrumbs, salt, pepper and thyme.
6. Add sufficient wine to bind the stuffing.
7. Pack the stuffing into the body cavities of the mackerel, fasten by threading a cocktail stick through.
8. Parcel each fish in foil, dotted with remaining butter.
9. Bake in a moderate oven (gas No. 4, 180 degrees C, 350F) for 30-40 minutes or until the fish is cooked and the flesh is white.
10. Serve garnished with apple rings and parsley.

Jaki Moore, Sompting

Selsey Sole

Serves 1

2	fillets lemon or Dover sole (skinned)
50g (2oz)	prawns
100g (2fl oz)	white wine
25g (1oz)	onion finely chopped
150ml (1/4 pt)	fish veloute
150ml (1/4 pt)	double cream
150ml (1/4 pt)	stock
1 teasp	chopped parsley
1	puff pastry fleuron

Fish Veloute

25g (1oz)	margarine
25g (1oz)	flour
150ml (1/4 pt)	fishstock

1. Poach fillets with onions, white wine and fish stock, until cooked.
2. Remove fish, reduce liquor.
3. Make fish veloute, by melting margarine, adding the flour, slightly cook and add fishstock stirring well.
4. Add fish veloute to liquor, reduce to thicken.
5. Add cream and gently simmer.
6. Add prawns, fish and garnish with fleuron and parsley.

Mark A Harwood, Brinsbury Est.

Cultivated Success

In the late 19th Century, Sussex became the cradle of cultivated mushroom production in Britain. Extensive natural supplies of excellent quality wild mushrooms were to be found in the Sussex Downlands. Flourishing horticultural centres, , such as Worthing and Littlehampton, already supplying the Victorian London markets with such "exotics" as hothouse grapes, provided the necessary expertise and enthusiasm to pioneer controlled mushroom production.

One pioneer of cultivated mushroom production was Arthur Linfield who founded in 1882 what is today Chesswood Produce. As an enterprising fruit grower and general farmer in Worthing, he found that the straw from his pig farm was ideal for protecting the roots of his glasshouse-produced grapes. To his surprise these ideal conditions resulted in the growth of "wild" mushrooms. He had discovered the technique for cultivated mushroom production. He collected spawn from the natural sites on the Downlands and, with several other enthusiasts, developed spawn which could be cultivated into a year-round mushroom crop.

By the 1920s his production techniques were so successful that Linfield moved to Thakeham, near Pulborough, and grew mushrooms as his main crop.

Mushrooms became more and more popular. To meet this demand, Linfields realised that by prepacking and fast delivery, fresh mushrooms could be on sale daily throughout the UK. By 1964 AG Linfield Ltd, which started as a small family business became the largest mushroom producer in the UK.

Today, Sussex growers account for some 46 per cent of UK production and are still the leaders in innovation and investment in their future. Many have remained specialists, but the largest have expanded and merged over the years perhaps inevitably in modern market conditions, and have become parts of large food groups - thus, Chesswood Produce is now part of Rank Hovis McDougall (RHM). The Linfield heritage combines well with RHM's commitment to research and development of this rapidly growing market which, since the early 1980s has doubled in size. In 1988 Chesswood's annual production was over 130,000 tonnes - that is enough for a half pound bag of mushrooms for every person in the country!.

Chesswood supplies the majority of the major supermarket chains and wholesale markets as

well as the catering and processing trade. The mushroom crops have to be controlled to coincide with these market demands. Modern scale production therefore requires sophisticated and flexible co-ordination of growing, harvesting, packaging, transportation and distribution. Within 16 hours Chesswood mushrooms are picked, weighed, packed and dispatched. The whole process takes place daily in a modern, air-condtioned, temperature-controlled environment.

Chesswood currently produces a whole range of quality fresh mushrooms, from small buttons to large flats, of a cultivated variety related to the large field mushroom, and increasingly a new organically grown variety, the "brown cap" or "chestnut" mushroom.

Chesswood's Recipes for you

Mushroom Cream Flan

Serve dainty slices as a hot hors d'oeuvre, larger ones as a main course with salad, or take it cold as picnic fare.

125g (4 oz.) each of wholemeal flour, plain flour and block margarine, 250g (8 oz.) open flat mushrooms, 25g (1 oz.) butter or margarine. 2 whole eggs and 1 egg yolk, 150g (5 fl. oz.) carton natural yoghurt, 90ml (6 tbsp.) single cream, salt and freshly ground black pepper. A little grated nutmeg, 30ml (2 level tbsp.) snipped chives.

Prepare the shortcrust pastry and roll out to line a 23cm (9 in.) loose-bottomed flan tin. Bake "blind" at 190°C (375°F) mark 5 until just beginning to colour. Meanwhile wipe mushrooms and slice. Sauté them in the hot fat in a frying pan for a few minutes only to seal, and drain. Whisk the whole eggs, egg yolk, yoghurt, cream, nutmeg, seasoning and chives together. Scatter the mushrooms over the base of the flan case, pour over the custard mixture and bake at 190°C (375°F) mark 5 for about 30 min., or until just set and golden brown.
Serves 6 hot or cold.

Lamb Casserole with Mushroom Dumplings

A hearty, nourishing dish that's just a little bit different.

45ml (3 tbsp.) oil, 1 medium onion, skinned and sliced, 900g (2 lb.) middle neck lamb, cut up, 45ml (3 level tbsp.) flour, 400ml (¾ pint) stock, 400g (14 oz.) can tomatoes, 10ml (2 level tsp.) paprika, 5ml (1 level tsp.) salt, freshly ground black pepper.
Dumplings:
125g (4 oz.) cup mushrooms, wiped, 125g (4 oz.) self-raising flour, 50g (2 oz.) shredded suet, 15ml (1 tbsp.) chopped parsley, 5ml (1 level tsp.) salt, freshly ground black pepper, water to mix. Serves 4.

Heat the oil, fry the onion to soften then add the lamb and brown quickly. Stir in flour and cook 1 min. Gradually stir in stock, tomatoes and juice, and seasonings. Bring to the boil, stirring. Transfer to an ovenproof dish, cover and cook at 170°C (325°F) mark 3 for 2 hr. Turn oven temperature up to 200°C (400°F) mark 6. Dumplings: chop mushrooms quite coarsely and stir into the dry ingredients. Mix with water to give a soft dough. Shape into 8 dumplings and add to casserole. Cover and return to the oven for 20-25 min.

Golden Fish Supper

Cook tomato halves alongside this dish in the oven and serve together with hot finger rolls. Try it topped with breadcrumbs instead of potato crisps.

250-375g (8-12 oz.) closed mushrooms, 450g (1 lb.) coley, 65g (2½ oz.) butter or margarine, 45ml (3 level tbsp.) flour, 300ml (½ pint) milk, 45ml (3 tbsp.) chopped parsley, salt and freshly ground black pepper, 30 ml (2 tbsp.) lemon juice. Small pkt. potato crisps, 50g (2 oz.) grated cheddar cheese.
Serves 4.

Wipe and quarter the mushrooms. Skin the fish, cut into 2.5cm (1 in.) pieces and lightly brown in 40g (1½ oz.) fat in a frying pan and sauté for 2-3 min; drain well and mix with the fish. Meanwhile make a white sauce with the remaining fat, flour, milk, parsley and seasoning. Add the lemon juice without reboiling. Pour into the pie dish.
Top with roughly crushed potato crisps and cheese mixed together and bake at 190°C (375°F) mark 5 for about 30 min., or until golden brown on top.

Crusty Mushroom Rolls

Hey presto! Creamed mushrooms in a new guise - just the thing for impromptu gatherings. Equally delicious on thick hot toast or spooned into feather-light warm pastry cases.

250g (8 oz.) button mushrooms, 25g (1 oz.) butter or margarine, 15ml (1 level tbsp.) flour, 142ml (5 fl. oz.) carton single cream, 30ml (2 tbsp.) chopped parsley, salt and freshly ground black pepper, 30ml (2 tbsp.) sherry, 4 large crusty rolls, 25g (1 oz.) melted butter.

Wipe button mushrooms. Sauté the mushrooms in the hot fat for 2-3 min. until well browned. Remove from heat, stir in flour, cream, parsley and seasoning. Bring to the boil and simmer gently for 2 min., stirring. Add sherry without reboiling.
Cut the tops off the rolls and carefully scoop out the crumbs, leaving a 0.5cm (¼ in.) thick "shell". Brush the insides of the rolls with melted butter, spoon in the mushroom filling, replace tops and bake at 190°C (375°F) mark 5 for 15 min. Makes 4.

Nearly all the mushrooms we buy in this country are a close relative of the common field mushroom. Despite their consistent quality and absolute safety, there are still some people who argue that wild mushrooms are superior – perhaps they have never tasted the fully mature cultivated ones that are available in the shops.

Mushrooms have a lot in their favour. Besides being particularly tasty, both cooked and raw, they are one of the few foods with which there need be no waste.

They are rich in B vitamins, have traces of iron and other minerals and are great for slimmers as they contain no fat or carbohydrate and provide only 12 calories per 100 g. – as long as they aren't cooked in butter, of course!

For further information about mushrooms and their uses write to:
Chesswood Produce Ltd., Thakeham, Pulborough, West Sussex. RH20 3EL.

Three Days in June.....
and Much More

The South of England Agricultural Society is probably best known for its three day South of England Show held in June each year, attracting more than 100,000 visitors to Ardingly. However, the work of the Society does not end with the annual show, as the South of England Centre has an established calendar of agricultural and equestrian events throughout the year.

In 1988 the opening of the Norfolk Pavilion enabled the Society to enter the field of

The Norfolk Pavilion

conferences, exhibitions and banqueting. Set in the attractive surroundings of the 150 acre Centre, the Pavilion offers a choice of five interconnecting rooms on two floors, catering for 20 to 500 people and offering a unique venue for a wide variety of events.

Regular craft and antiques fairs are held at the Centre and many companies find the facilities ideal for trade launches or corporate hospitality days for clients and staff when they can fully utilise the spacious grounds for country pursuits such as clay pigeon shooting or fly fishing.

Despite this expansion into more commercial acti-

vities, Agriculture and Education play an important part in the work of the Society. Projects such as the 'Farmer Adopt a School' scheme give children the opportunity to learn about the operation of a farm and to witness seasonal changes in the farmers' work. Competitions are run for both agricultural and non-agricultural students and the Society also sponsors special projects on subjects such as organic farming. 'Eurolink' exchanges give British farmers the opportunities to exchange ideas with their European counterparts while further afield the Society is currently sponsoring VSO projects in Tanzania and Nepal.

Conferences and seminars are regularly organised by the Society the latest of which was run in conjunction with Nuffield Scholars and, topically, was entitled 'Food - producing for the Consumer'.

The South of England Agricultural Society welcomes new members from all disciplines not just those directly involved in agriculture, horticulture or equestrian activities. Membership means that you contribute to the educational and development work of the Society as well as obtaining free admission and parking for all three days of the Show, plus reduced admission to other events.

If you would like to become a member and support the Society's work, please telephone (0444) 892700 for further details.

The South of England Show

Seahaven Bounty

Serves 6

6	large scallops
12g (1/2oz)	butter
12g (1/2oz)	onion, finely diced
25g (1oz)	carrot, peeled, sliced and cut into fine strips
50g (2oz)	broccoli spears or asparagus tips, cut into bite sized pieces
350g (14oz)	puff pastry
	egg wash
3 sheets	Nori leaves (Japanese seaweed available from health food shops)
	Blanched spinach leaves can be used instead

Mousseline fish mousse can be made with a variety of seafoods

200g (8oz)	flounder, dab or whiting fillets
200g (8oz)	monkfish, bream, scallops, lobster coral and meat (if available)
1	egg
1	egg white
1 teasp	anchovy essence
	salt and pepper for seasoning
300ml (12fl oz)	double cream
1 tablesp	chopped fresh herbs; parsley, tarragon, chives etc.

Sauce

250ml (10fl oz)	medium dry rose wine
150ml (6fl oz)	fish or vegetable stock
25g (1oz)	onion, finely chopped
25g (1oz)	butter, unsalted
75ml (3fl oz)	double cream or sour cream
	seasoning and chopped herbs
	arrowroot mixed with a little water

1. Plunge the scallops into a saucepan of boiling water for 10 secs to seal in the juices, remove, drain and pat dry with absorbent paper.
2. Heat the butter and stir fry the onions, carrots and broccoli until lightly cooked, remove from the pan and allow to cool.
3. Place all the seafood for the mousseline in a food processor and blend to a smooth paste with the eggs, anchovy essence and seasoning, take care to keep the mixture cool at all times.
4. Pass the mixture through a fine sieve then whisk in the double cream and herbs, beating until all is absorbed and the mixture is the texture of thickly beaten cream. Chill.
5. Divide the pastry in half and roll each piece into a rectangle 2.5mm (1/8in) thick, 250mm (10in) long by 100mm (4in) wide.
6. Place one rectangle of pastry onto an oiled baking sheet, cover with 2 sheets of Nori seaweed, with the excess evenly distributed down each side.
7. Spread a thin layer of seafood mousseline onto the seaweed within 15mm (1/2in) of the edge of the pastry.
8. Combine the blanched scallops and stir fried vegetables with a little of the mousseline and arrange down the centre of the base.
9. Cover with the remaining mousseline and shape into a semicircle.
10. Cut the remaining sheet of seaweed in half and with the excess fold up along each side to completely cover the filling.
11. To make the pastry cage cut 25mm (1in) long incisions alternately down the pastry
12. Shape the pastry over the filling, seal the edges and glaze with beaten egg.
13. Bake Gas No.7, 220 degrees C, 425F, for 10 mins then reduce the heat to medium and cook for a further 15-20 mins.
14. To make the sauce, fry the onions in the butter until soft, pour in the wine and stock and bring to the boil. Remove the scum and reduce the liquid by half, season and thicken with a little blended arrowroot. Remove from the heat and add the cream and chopped herbs.

Colin John Capon, Seaford

Conger Eel Curry

Serves 4

1 kilo (2 lbs)	conger eel
	vinegar
1	large onion - chopped
25g (1 oz)	butter
2 teasp	flour
2 teasp	curry powder
1 teasp	tomato puree
	dry white wine
	bouquet garni
	ginger root
	mace
1	egg yolk
2 tablesp	cream or milk

1. Skin and bone the eel, put in a dish and cover with equal parts of vinegar and water, with a little salt, and leave for 1 hour.
2. Saute the onion in butter, add the flour and curry powder and cook for a few minutes.
3. Add the tomato puree
4. Rinse the eel and cut into small pieces.
5. Place the eel in the pan with 3 parts water to 1 part wine to cover, add bouquet garni, ginger and mace.
6. Cover and simmer gently until eel is cooked.
7. Blend together the egg yolk and cream, add this to the pan, off the heat and shake pan to blend all together.
8. Remove the bouquet garni, mace and ginger.
9. Serve with rice.

Mrs P Huggins, Littlehampton

Trout and Prawn Galantine

Serves 5

200g (1/2 lb)	trout - cooked with bones removed
200g (1/2 lb)	prawns (or shrimps)
1 packet	aspic jelly
1 glass	sherry
	salt and pepper
150ml (1/4 pt)	double cream - lightly whipped
	cucumber slices

1. Flake trout and mix with prawns.
2. Melt aspic jelly in hot water, add fish mixture, sherry and seasoning.
3. When jelly is almost cold, stir in cream.
4. Put mixture in mould or individual dishes and chill.
5. Garnish with cucumber.

Jean Dann, Whatlington

The Sussex Brewers

The County Town of Lewes once boasted nine breweries; today only Harvey's Brewery remains.

The name of Harvey has long been associated with the supply of beers, wines and spirits in Sussex.

Records of 1794 recall the delivery of Old Red Port, Sherry and Claret within a twenty mile radius of Lewes. However, it was under the management of John Harvey (1784-1862) that the Bridge Wharf Brewery was established on its present site by the River Ouse.

The Brew House and Tower, which dominate the scene from Cliffe Bridge, were the result of re-building in 1880 and constitute a beautiful example of a country brewery in Victorian Gothic design. Today it remains an independent family firm with a 7th generation of Harvey's descendents actively involved in its affairs.

Selecting the finest quality Pale and Mild Ale Malts, together with the choicest Kent and Sussex hops, and brewing from their own fresh spring water and a yeast which has remained unchanged in the brewery for over three decades, has resulted in a range of beers

which have delighted the people of Sussex and Kent for many years. These beers have been the recipients of no less than fifteen major awards at International Brewers' Exhibitions and the brewery's reputation far exceeds the borders of its native county.

Their famous traditional Sussex Bitter, Old Ale and Elizabethan Ale barley wine are foremost

among a portfolio of five draught and ten bottled beers which may be found at numerous outlets throughout Sussex and Kent.

Although the oldest brewery in Sussex, Harvey's success is built on their willingness to innovate while retaining traditional values. This year has seen the launch of two low alcohol products, John Hop Low Alcohol Sussex Bitter and Bill Brewer Low Alcohol Sussex Old.

The firm are long established wine and spirit merchants and their shop at 6 Cliffe High Street, Lewes stocks their complete range of beers, together with a large selection of brewery souvenirs.

Goodwood: 300 Years of Hospitality

Since 1793 when the then Duke of Richmond created the Royal Horse Artillery in the Park, Goodwood has been the place to launch new products and services!. Happily, in the 1980's most such launches at Goodwood are less war-like. From telephones and motor cars to banking services and new share issues, Goodwood is used by national and international companies for those promotional events where the host accepts nothing but the best.

The 1st Duke of Richmond (much the least reliable of the line) bought old Goodwood House (completing payment only after threats of legal action!). From that day to this the estate has grown in size and richness as the hospitality offered has grown in opulence. In the 1980s these advantages are offered to commercial firms and private hosts alike, in the State Apartments which have been subtly adapted to match today's professional requirements. With some 200 events last year, Goodwood House is more alive and busier than at any time in the last 200 years.

Goodwood House, Goodwood Racecourse and Goodwood Park Hotel

The 3rd Duke started horse racing at Goodwood in 1801. He might well have been surprised to find that Goodwood Racecourse now boasts a huge grandstand and at the July meeting, approximately 100 private company entertainment pavilions.

Goodwood Park Hotel (90 Bedrooms) at the gate to Goodwood House, accommodates many people and firms using other Goodwood activities. But with its fine restaurant (The Dukes') and its own conference rooms, Leisure Centre and Golf Course, Goodwood Park Hotel has a flourishing and up-market corporate clientele of its own.

The Goodwood Aerodrome is the wartime Westhampnett Airfield - launching pad for Spitfires on D-Day. Around it runs the old Goodwood Motor Circuit. The Circuit is now used for demonstrations and testing. The Aerodrome is used by company aircraft and the Goodwood Flying Club.

Dressage at Goodwood and National and International Championships annually, offer opportunity for commercial entertaining and sponsorship. This is the latest chapter in the story of the Horse at Goodwood.Further information on all Goodwood Activities from The Group Relations Manager, Goodwood House, Goodwood, Chichester, West Sussex PO18 0PX Tel: (0243) 774107.

Plaice or Sole stuffed with Herb and Garlic Cheese

Serves 4

4	large fillets of fresh plaice or sole
300ml (1/2 pt)	water
	salt and pepper
100g (4 oz)	Sussex Slipcote herb and garlic cheese
25g (1 oz)	butter
25g (1 oz)	flour
4 teasp	tomato puree

1. Place fillets in a pan with water and seasoning and poach for 5 minutes.
2. Strain, retaining the liquor.
3. Carefully roll the fillets round a portion of the herb and garlic cheese and keep the fillets hot.
4. Melt the butter, add the flour and cook the roux. Make a coating sauce using the tomato puree and the fish liquor.
5. Coat the fillets with the sauce and serve.

Mrs G St J Hardy, Duddleswell

Brook Trout

Serves 2

4	rashers streaky bacon - rind removed
2	medium trout - cleaned
	salt and pepper
2 tablesp	lemon juice
1 tablesp	fresh chives

1. Place bacon in an ovenproof casserole and lay well seasoned trout on top.
2. Pour oven lemon juice and add chives.
3. Cook in a moderate over (Gas No. 4, 180 degrees C, 350F) for 15-20 minutes until the fish is cooked.

Neil Cruttenden, Uckfield Community College

This recipe was used by Neil to cook the trout that he caught on a rod and line from a Sussex lake; they weighed 1 lb 10 oz and 2 lbs 4 oz respectively.

Baked Codling

Serves 8

2-3 kilo (4-6 lb)	codling
100g (4 oz)	wholemeal breadcrumbs
50g (2 oz)	suet - chopped
1 tablesp	parsley - chopped
teasp	mixed herbs
lemon	rind - grated
1	egg - beaten
	salt and pepper
	milk

(breadcrumbs, suet, parsley, mixed herbs, lemon rind, egg, salt and pepper, milk } forcemeat)

1. Remove the heads, clean and wash the codling. Dry the inside.
2. Prepare forcemeat by mixing the ingredients together.
3. Fill the cavity of the fish with forcemeat and place it in a buttered roasting tin.
4. Pour over a little milk and cover with foil.
5. Bake in a moderate oven (Gas No.4, 180 degrees C, 350F) for 50 mins.

Mrs Edith Tucker, Brighton

Poultry, Meat and Game

It is not surprising that a number of original lamb recipes were submitted for the competition as Sussex is famous for its Southdown sheep and Sussex cattle, both of which are bred for meat. Poultry and rabbits are farmed for the table and this meat, low in fat is proving to be popular with those who strive to eat a healthy diet.

Lamb and Bean Paprika

Serves 4

400g (1lb)	tomatoes, skinned and chopped
300ml (1/2 pt)	chicken stock
400g (1lb)	boned and trimmed leg of lamb cut into 2 cm (1 in) cubes
200g (8 oz)	mixed beans and pulses according to season (e.g. French and haricot beans and sweetcorn) or canned, dried or frozen if out of season
1 medium	onion, chopped
1 clove	garlic, crushed
1/2	red pepper, sliced
100g (4 oz)	button mushrooms
1 teasp	chopped parsley
1/2 teasp	oregano
1/4 teasp	cumin powder
2 teasp	paprika pepper
dash	worcester sauce
25g (1 oz)	cornflour
50ml (2 fl oz)	white wine
100ml (4 fl oz)	yoghurt (Sussex Sheeps milk)

1. Heat the tomatoes and stock in a large pan until boiling, add the cubed lamb and seal in the hot liquid.
2. Add the vegetables, spices and seasonings.
3. Transfer to a large casserole and cook in a moderate oven, Gas No. 5, 190 degrees C, 375F, for 1 1/2-2 1/2 hours until the lamb is tender and the vegetables cooked.
4. Thicken the casserole using the cornflour blended with wine; adjust seasoning.
5. Serve in a clean casserole with the yoghurt poured over.

Janet Anthony, Plumpton

Southdown Lamb Roulade

Serves 4

2	lamb fillets
250g (10 oz)	streaky bacon
2 tablesp	herbs - freshly chopped (coriander, thyme, marjoram & parsley)
100g (4 oz)	breadcrumbs
1 clove	garlic - crushed
1 small	onion - grated
2 tablesp	redcurrant jelly
	olive oil

1. Trim the fillets and place together.
2. Lay the trimmed bacon on a board, overlapping, to form a rectangle the length of the meat.
3. Mix the herbs with the breadcrumbs, garlic and onion.
4. Coat the fillet with the jelly and roll in the breadcrumbs.
5. Place the coated meat on the bacon and roll up like a Swiss roll.
6. Secure the roll with cocktail sticks and tie firmly with string.
7. Brush the roulade with olive oil and either cook on a hot barbecue for 20-30 minutes, turning at 10 minute intervals or roast in a hot oven (Gas No. 7, 220 degrees C, 425F) for 30-40 minutes depending on the size of the fillets.

Mrs Mary Stewart, Barns Green

Palace Extraordinaire

The Royal Pavilion, one of the most extraordinary palaces in the world, is certainly the most dazzling and exotic in the British Isles. This dream-like fantastic summer palace is a breathtaking experience and one of Britain's most important works of art. In it, George, Prince of Wales, lived as Regent and as King, gathering about himself a brilliant and cultivated society. One of the most frequent visitors was Mrs Fitzherbert, to whom he was secretly married in 1785. To it the news of Trafalgar and of other victories of the Napoleonic period were first brought.

The Prince of Wales began building the Royal Pavilion in 1787, and thenceforth it was gradually enlarged and elaborated, each time in a more rich, strange and sumptuous style. Its present form dates largely from 1815 to 1822 when it was rebuilt by Nash in the 'Indian' style. The interiors were decorated in the 'Chinese taste', which was here carried to unique heights of splendour and magnificence. On it the Prince lavished enormous sums.

In recent years, the magnificent interior decorations have been restored. Varnish discoloured by time has been removed, revealing original colours in their former brilliance. Victorian decorations have been replaced by faithful re-creation in the original colour and designs; original mouldings, lanterns, fittings and furniture have been restored to their proper positions.

Throughout the year most of the State and Pri-

vate Apartments are fully arranged with furniture, carpets, porcelain and other works of art of the late 18th and early 19th centuries, from the permanent collection of the Royal Pavilion, which is one of the most comprehensive of its period in the country. In particular, the dazzling Banqueting Room is set out, as for a royal banquet, with the most sumptuous display of Regency silver-gilt on show anywhere.

Brighton itself still has beautiful Regency buildings and a splendid, largely period sea front. The Royal Pavilion is not more than five minutes' walk from Brighton Station. It is open daily 10am to 5pm including Sundays, October to May except Christmas; from early June to end of September, 10am to 6pm.

Guide services for parties are available on application to The Keeper of Public Services, The Royal Pavilion, Brighton BN1 IUE. Tel (0273) 603005.

The Great Kitchen

The Answer lies in the Soil

One of the reasons for the rural unrest in the 1830s was said to be the high rate of illiteracy among farm workers. To alleviate the problem, agricultural schools were started in East Dean, Jevington, Lindfield and Brighton.

At Lindfield, each boy looked after one-eighth of an acre and grew oats, turnips, mangels and potatoes. Half their produce was handed in as rent, the rest they were allowed to sell. This

scheme was to try and overcome the reluctance of agricultural workers to send their sons on courses "when they could be earning money". The schools strengthened their argument by saying that proper training would make them 'more useful'.

In 1889 The Technical Instruction Act enabled the new schools to establish a penny rate (0.24p) to provide finance for a new school at Uckfield and a 'Migratory Butter Making School' travelled the county staying at farms for a few weeks at a time to give instruction in butter and cheese-making.

Plumpton College was opened in 1926 with courses covering dairying, machinery, beekeeping, stock rearing, fencing and hedging. Before 1913 there was little formal agricultural education in West Sussex but that year the County Council placed an advertisement for an Agricultural Organiser offering a salary of £300 with an allowance of 7p for lunch, 12p for dinner and bed and breakfast at 30p.

Throughout the 20s and 30s there were experiments and lectures on clean milk, poultry, horticulture and beekeeping and in 1940 this work was transferred to the Brinsbury Estate under the auspices of the War Agricultural Executive. In 1951 the estate was bought by WSCC for an Agricultural College but the Ministry of Agriculture refused permission. So the county ran its own training school until 1965 when the Ministry of Education recognised the need for an agricultural education centre in West Sussex and gave its blessing to the development.

During the war, both Brinsbury and Plumpton were used as training centres for the Women's Land Army and thousands came on one month courses. Afterwards, until 1951, the War Office took over the premises to retrain ex-service personnel.

Today, a wide range of courses is available at both colleges. Traditional Agricultural and commercial horticulture are still provided either on a full time or day release basis. Other options include such diverse courses as floristry, woodland skills, turf culture, blacksmithing, horse husbandry and management, goat keeping and the care of small animals.

More information from: Plumpton Agricultural College, Nr Lewes, East Sussex. Tel: (0273) 890454; and West Sussex College of Agriculture and Horticulture, Brinsbury, North Heath, Nr Pulborough, West Sussex. Tel:(07982) 3832.

Posies of Lamb

Serves 3

1	loin of lamb - boned - save fillet mignon
100g (4oz)	shallots - finely chopped
50g (2oz)	butter
150g (6 oz)	blackcurrants
1/2	small white loaf - crumbed
50g (2 oz)	fennel - cut into fine strips and blanched seasoning
1 glass	mead
1 teasp	redcurrant jelly
3 sprigs	fennel

1. Prepare stuffing by sweating shallots in 25g (1 oz) butter, without colouring.
2. Add half blackcurrants, fry for 1 minute, remove from heat.
3. Stir in breadcrumbs and blanched fennel strips, season.
4. Spread stuffing on underside of loin, place on fillet mignon.
5. Roll and tie with 6 strings.
6. Divide lamb between strings to give 6 even pieces.
7. Melt remaining butter in a frying pan and gently fry the posies until pink, transfer to serving dish.
8. Add the mead to the pan and stir in the redcurrant jelly. Add the remaining blackcurrants and reduce sauce, pour over posies
9. Garnish with sprigs of fennel.

Jerry Cowell, Eastbourne

Lamb on the Green

Serves 4-6

1	small leg of lamb - boned
Stuffing	
100g (4 oz)	fresh breadcrumbs
1	small onion - chopped
1	small apple - chopped
50g (2 oz)	butter - softened
	parsley - chopped
	salt and black pepper
200g (8 oz)	mushrooms - sliced
1/2 kilo (1 lb)	courgettes - sliced
3 hpd tablesp	chopped mint
3 hpd tablesp	chopped parsley

1. Combine stuffing ingredients and stuff lamb cavity, tie with string.
2. Weigh stuffed lamb and calculate roasting time at 75 minutes per kilo (35 minutes per lb.)
3. Roast lamb in shallow tin until 35 minutes from end of cooking time at Gas No. 5, 190 degrees C, 375F.
4. Remove meat from tin.
5. Add sliced mushrooms and courgettes and stir to incorporate meat juices. Replace lamb on top and complete cooking.
6. Carve lamb into thick slices, keep hot.
7. Stir mint and parsley into roasting tin.
8. Make a bed of vegetables on serving dish and place lamb slices down centre, overlapping neatly.
9. Serve with rosemary jelly.

Mrs B L Taylor, Barns Green

Liver Stroganoff

Serves 4

2	onions, peeled and sliced
1 tablesp	oil
100g (4 oz)	mushrooms
500g (1lb)	lambs liver, cut into strips and floured
250ml (1/2pt)	stock
100ml (3 fl. oz.)	red wine
	Top of the milk, yoghurt or soured single cream

1.	Fry onions in oil, add mushrooms and brown lightly.
2.	Remove vegetables from pan, add liver and fry for a few minutes.
3.	Return vegetables, add stock & wine, simmer for 15 minutes.
4.	Remove from heat and stir in milk or yoghurt or cream.

Mrs V M King, Bexhill-on-Sea

Galantine of Beef

Serves 6

1 kilo (2 lbs)	lean minced beef
100g (4 oz)	bacon (minced)
1 tablesp	ketchup - mushroom or tomato
1/4 teasp	mixed spice
1 tablesp	chopped parsley
1 tablesp	chopped chives
2	eggs - beaten
	salt and pepper
150g (6 oz)	breadcrumbs

1.	Mix all the ingredients together with the exception of the breadcrumbs.
2.	Press firmly into greased tins and bake in a moderate oven (Gas No. 5, 190 degrees C, 375F) for 1 1/2 hours.
3.	Turn out carefully and roll in breadcrumbs, serve cold with salad.

This mixture can be boiled for 3 hours in a loosely tied, floured pudding cloth.

Mrs D L Murless, North Lancing

Spicy Sausages

Serves 2

Spicy Sausages with Horsham Hedgehog

25g (1 oz)	butter
200g (1/2 lb)	Sussex pork sausages (skinned)
2 rashers	streaky bacon (chopped)
1 medium	onion (finely chopped)
1 level teaspoon	mustard (made up)
2 tablesp	tomato ketchup
1 level tablesp	chutney
	salt, pepper and pinch cayenne pepper
2	tomatoes peeled and quartered

1.	Melt butter in pan, add chopped sausages, streaky bacon and onion, fry gently for about 5 minutes.
2.	Stir in remaining ingredients, heat and serve.

This recipe was used in East Grinstead over 80 years ago.

Mr D Allen, South Lancing

Iron Horses

Advances in the technology of agricultural machinery have played a very large part in the transformation of agriculture from a labour intensive industry, where a large percentage of food was imported, to an industry where less than 3% of the population provides more than 80% of the food that can be grown in the UK.

Famous pioneers of agricultural machinery include Jethro Tull who invented the seed drill in the 1700s and much later Harry Ferguson who introduced the now famous 'grey fergie' in the 1940s. The farm implements that existed prior to the early 1900s were horse-drawn and although tractors began to appear on farms in greater numbers during the 1920s, there were still thousands  of horses on Sussex farms at the outbreak of the last war.

Prior to the turn of the century, scythes were the means of cutting standing corn. The first 'mechanised reaper' came to Sussex in the late 1890s but harvesting was still labour intensive with women and children following the reaper to tie the corn into sheaves. Sheaves were stacked into stooks prior to transporting to the farmyard in large horse-drawn Sussex wagons.

During the autumn and winter steam engine driven threshing tackle separated the grain from the straw. Threshing machinery was still in use on farms in Sussex albeit on a limited scale in the late 1950s.

Despite the fact that a labour intensive agriculture involved long arduous hours, often in filthy conditions which would not be tolerated today, farm staff viewed the march of mechanisation with mixed feelings; the first self tying reaper was burnt by labourers who feared their jobs were in jeopardy.

Many of the early farm implements were built locally by the village blacksmith and other local agricultural engineers. Records show that in 1912 a Horsham agricultural engineer named Walter Wood manufactured his own reaper-binder and several were used locally.

With the advent of the internal combustion engine manufacture of tractors became a major industrialised operation. Large numbers of tractors came to Sussex during the War as part of the 'lease-lend' arrangements.

Many smaller manufacturers of tractors are no longer with us, today and the tractor market, as with the motor car market, is dominated by Fords who are the only manufacturer who produce substantial numbers of tractors in Britain. They are represented in Sussex by Sussex Tractors Ltd machinery dealers who have served the farming industry in Sussex for almost 50 years.

Anyone who visits their showrooms, stores and workshops at Uckfield or Horsham, cannot fail to be impressed with the advances in the range of agricultural machinery and in tractor design that have occurred over the last 70 years.

Sussex Tractors main office is at 33 New Town, Uckfield, East Sussex TN22 5DL.
Tel: (0825) 2112.

The Weald and Downland Open Air Museum

The Weald & Downland Open Air Museum started in 1967. Its principal aim has been to establish a centre that could rescue representative examples of threatened vernacular buildings from south-east England. So far more than thirty buildings have been reconstructed and a large number are in store. In addition the Museum has established a collection of artefacts representing country crafts and industries, building trades and agriculture. These are, and will be, used to furnish buildings and act as exhibits in their own right.

Some of the many interesting exhibits to be seen on the Museum's 40 acre Downland site include 15th, 16th and 17th century houses, farm buildings, rural craft workshops, a Tudor market hall, a village school and the Lurgashall watermill. The mill is in daily operation during the summer and is well known for its stone-ground flour.

The Museum is a popular tourist attraction with ever changing exhibitions and special activities. For example, in 1989, the Museum hosted many of the activities celebrating British Food and Farming Year and opened a medieval farmstead and a History of Farming Exhibition. The farmstead is centred around the 15th century Bayleaf farmhouse and a late medieval barn from Cowfold. The house is furnished and surrounded by a garden and orchard to complete the picture of the late medieval domestic life. The farmstead has livestock and is equipped, using replica medieval tools and implements, demonstrating how it might have looked. The History of Farming Exhibition shows how agriculture has changed and developed in the south-east from medieval times to the present day.

Also opened in 1989 was a permanent History of Brickmaking Exhibition. Regular annual events include sheepdog trials in May, working demonstrations of heavy horses in June, the well established Show for Rare Breeds in July and the Steam Threshing and Ploughing weekend in October.

The Museum is a charitable trust and its advancement over the last twenty years has been made possible by the support of many individuals, trusts and companies. Its pattern of continually adding new buildings makes return visits especially interesting.

The Museum is at Singleton, nr Chichester, West Sussex PO18 0EU. Tel: (024363) 348. Open April 1st to October 31st daily, 11am to 5pm. November 1st to March 31st, Weds, Suns and Bank Holidays 11am to 4pm.

Bayleaf Farmhouse

WEALD&DOWNLAND OPEN AIR MUSEUM

Chicken Pie

Serves 6-8

2 kilo (4 lb)	chicken - boiled
350g (14 oz)	plain flour
100g (4 oz)	lard
50g (2 oz)	butter
50g (2 oz)	strong cheese - grated
1 teasp	mustard - mixed
400g (1 lb)	sausagemeat
1 teasp	fresh herbs - chopped (sage and savoury)
	or 1/2 teasp dried herbs
1	egg - beaten
2 tablesp	cooking oil
200g (8 oz)	shallots - chopped (or 400g (1lb) onions)
200g (8oz)	mushrooms
200g (8 oz)	streaky bacon
2	eggs - hard boiled and sliced

cheese shortcrust pastry (brace spanning plain flour, lard, butter, strong cheese, mustard)

1. Remove flesh from bones of chicken, set aside.
2. Make cheese shortcrust pastry, chill.
3. Mix sausagemeat with herbs and beaten egg and line a 2 litre (4 pt) pie dish with this mixture.
4. Place chunks of chicken over sausagemeat.
5. Fry the shallots/onions and mushrooms in oil, add to pie.
6. Fry bacon until brown and place on top of the pie, cover with the hard boiled eggs.
7. Add a little stock to moisten.
8. Roll out the cheese pastry and cover the pie, glaze.
9. Bake in a moderate oven (Gas No. 4, 180 degrees C, 350F) for 40 minutes.

Eileen O'Neill, Worthing

Pheasant with Bacon Rolls and Calvados Sauce

Serves 4

2	pheasants - prepared
1	onion - chopped
1 teasp	crushed juniper berries
300ml (1/2 pt)	red wine
600ml (1 pt)	chicken stock
450ml (3/4 pt)	pheasant stock
8 rashers	streaky bacon
200g (8 oz)	mushrooms
onion - chopped	
300ml (1/2 pt)	double cream
4 tablesp	calvados

1. Put one chopped onion in a roasting dish and place portions of pheasant on top.
2. Add juniper berries, red wine and chicken stock, cover with foil and braise in a moderate oven (gas No. 5, 190 degrees C, 375F) for 1 3/4 hours.
3. When cold, remove pheasant portions and separate the meat from the bone.
4. Place meat in a clean dish. Put the skin and bones in a saucepan with water and prepare 450ml (3/4 pt) pheasant stock.
5. Make 16 bacon rolls from streaky bacon and fry gently, add to pheasant.
6. Saute second onion and mushrooms in bacon fat and add to dish.
7. Pour on cream, calvados and strained pheasant stock, cover.
8. Return to moderate oven for 30-40 minutes.

Lucy Ann, Alfriston

Sussex Chicken

Serves 2

25g (1 oz)	butter
1 clove	garlic - crushed
25g (1 oz)	cheese - grated
1 bag	ready salted crisps - crushed
2	chicken breasts - skinned

1. Heat butter and garlic in a small pan.
2. Mix the cheese and crisps on a plate.
3. Brush the chicken breasts with melted butter and coat with cheese and crisp mixture.
4. Place chicken on a baking sheet and pour over remaining butter. Pile left over cheese and crisps on top.
5. Cook in a moderate oven (Gas No. 5, 190 degrees C, 375F) for 45 minutes.

Debbie Chambers, Dorothy Stringer High School, Brighton

Drunken Chicken

Serves 8

2 kilo (4 lb)	fresh chicken, jointed into 8 pieces
50g (2 oz)	flour
1/2 teasp	black pepper
1/2 teasp	marjoram
1/2 teasp	fenugreek
1 teasp	salt
50g (2 oz)	butter
425ml (3/4 pt)	brandy
600ml (1 pt)	thick yoghurt (Sussex High Weald Dairy sheeps)
2	eggs
2 teasp	paprika
	a few sprigs of fresh parsley

1. Prepare seasoned flour by adding pepper, marjoram, fenugreek and salt.
2. Toss chicken joints in seasoned flour then fry them in melted butter until brown.
3. Place in a large casserole and add brandy, cook in a moderate oven Gas No. 4, 180 degrees C, 350F until tender.
4. Add beaten eggs to yoghurt, add to casserole and cook over a low heat for 5 minutes.
5. Serve sprinkled with paprika and garnished with parsley.

Mrs. G St J Hardy, Duddleswell

Lamb Conference

Serves 4

1 kilo (2 lbs)	leg of lamb - boned and cubed
25g (1 oz)	seasoned flour
2 tablesp	cooking oil
4	pears - peeled and quartered
200g (8 oz)	button mushrooms
100ml (4 fl oz)	stock
100ml (4 fl oz)	white wine
	seasoning

1. Toss the lamb cubes in seasoned flour, fry in hot oil until brown.
2. Add pears, mushrooms, stock, wine and seasoning; heat well.
3. Transfer to a casserole and cook in a moderate oven, Gas No. 4, 180 degrees C, 350F, for an hour or until the lamb is tender.

Margaret Green, Bexhill-on-Sea

Pork Slices with Barbecue Sauce

Serves 4

450g (1 lb)	lean British pork belly slices
1	onion chopped
1 tablesp	corn or sunflower oil
1 tablesp	tomato puree
2 teasps	white wine vinegar
300ml (1/2pt)	unsweetened orange juice
1 tablesp	brown sugar
1 tablesp	Worcestershire sauce

1. Cook the belly slices under a pre-heated grill for about 7 minutes each side, depending on thickness.
2. Meanwhile, saute the onion in the oil until softened.
3. Stir in the remaining ingredients and bring to the boil.
4. Simmer for 10 minutes. Service with boiled brown rice.

Meat & Livestock Commission

Beef with Honey and Ginger

Serves 4

4 x 175g (6oz)	British beef braising steaks
1 tablesp	corn or sunflower oil
2 teasp	fresh or dried rosemary
2	cloves garlic
1	2.5cm (1") piece of root ginger, peeled and finely chopped
100g (4oz)	mushrooms, sliced
1 tablesp	soy sauce
1 tablesp	clear honey
150ml (1/4pt)	stock
	black pepper

1. Heat the oil and brown the steaks on both sides.
2. Lay the steaks in an overproof dish large enough to place them side by side.
3. Mix the remaining ingredients together and pour over the beef.
4. Cover and cook in the oven Gas No 3, 170C, 325F for 90 minutes.
5. Serve with brown rice and a winter salad.

Meat & Livestock Commission

Herby Pork Burgers

Makes 8 burgers

450g (1 lb)	lean minced British pork
1	onion, finely chopped
50g (2oz)	hazelnuts, finely chopped
50g (2oz)	fresh wholemeal breadcrumbs
1 tablesp	sesame seeds
1 teasp	dried thyme
1 tablesp	chopped fresh parsley
	salt and pepper

1. Put all the ingredients together in a large bowl and mix well.
2. Divide the mixture into 8 equal portions and shape into burgers.
3. Cook either under a pre-heated grill or on a barbecue for about 5 - 7 minutes each side until cooked.
4. Serve with salad and wholemeal pitta.

Meat & Livestock Commission

Chilli Mince

Serves 4

450g (1lb)	lean minced British beef
1	onion, sliced
400g (14oz)	can red kidney beans, drained and rinsed
200g (7oz)	can baked beans
1 teasp	chilli powder
	salt
150ml (1/4pt)	stock
1 tablesp	cornflour
2 tablesp	water

1. Put the mince into a cold non-stick saucepan without adding fat and heat gently until some fat runs out.
2. Add the onion and increase the heat.
3. Continue to cook until the mince is brown and the onion softened.
4. Stir in the rest of the ingredients except the blended cornflour, bring to the boil, cover and simmer for 30 minutes.
5. Add the blended cornflour and cook, stirring until thickened. Serve with jacket potatoes.

Meat & Livestock Commission

Food for Thought

The Eastbourne College of Domestic Economy was founded in 1907 by Elise Orange Randall. Here, next to the seafront, students study for the highly acclaimed College Diploma.

In the first two terms, the Foundation Course has a strong emphasis on cookery but also includes catering, needlecraft, home and consumer studies, typing and child care.

In the third term, students specialise in Cordon Bleu cookery, catering and advanced dress. There is also a one term Intensive Cookery Course when student study for an Advanced Cordon Bleu Diploma.

This well-known College is residential with students commencing their courses in January or September. Having achieved their Eastbourne Diploma, students are well sought after by employers.

Members of the public are invited to visit the 'Rannies Restaurant' at the College. This is a teaching restaurant designed to give excellent practical experience in working as part of a team and cooking to deadlines.

Information about the Restaurant and the College is available from: Eastbourne College of Domestic Economy, 1 Silverdale Road, Eastbourne, East Sussex. Tel: (0323) 30851.

Downland Rabbit Pie

Serves 6

1	Sussex rabbit
100g (4 oz)	smoked bacon
100g (4oz)	sweetbreads (blanched and skinned)
1	small swede (chopped)
1	onion (chopped)
250ml (1/2 pt)	stock
1 teasp	freshly ground coriander
salt and pepper	
125ml (1/4 pt)	coating roux sauce made with milk
200g (8 oz)	shortcrust pastry
egg glaze	

Downland Rabbit Pie and Drunken Chicken

1. Simmer jointed rabbit with bacon, sweetbreads, swede and onion in stock to which coriander and seasoning have been added.
2. When cooked, cool and bone the rabbit and add the roux sauce to the other ingredients.
3. Place the rabbit mixture in a 1 litre (2 pt) pie dish and cover with shortcrust pastry. Glaze with egg.
4. Bake for 20 minutes at Gas No. 6, 200 degrees C, 400F, then lower to Gas 3, 160 degrees C, 325F for a further 20 minutes.

Mrs M Reeder, Pulborough

Romany Rabbit

Serves 6

1 kilo (2lbs)	rabbit joints
2-3 tablesp	cooking oil
4 rashers	streaky bacon (cut into pieces)
1 litre (2 pts.)	water
50g (2 oz)	raisins
4	small onions (chopped)
4	carrots (chopped)
1	clove garlic (crushed)
2	handfulls parsley roughly chopped
2 or 3	cloves
1	lemon (peel only)
1	turnip (chopped)
4	sticks celery (cut into 2cm (1in) pieces)
2	large tomatoes (skinned)
1	bouquet garni of rosemary, bay, thyme and sage
4 to 8	potatoes (cut into quarters)
1/2 tin	tomato soup or some tomato puree

1. Fry the rabbit joints in hot oil until browned, transfer to a 3 litre (6 pts) saucepan with a tight fitting lid.
2. Lightly fry streaky bacon and add to pan with all the other ingredients, bring to boil.
3. Simmer for at least 2 hours until the leg meat leaves the bone easily. Serve.

Christopher Fielder, Rye

Puddings and Desserts

The recipes for puddings and desserts reflects the predominence of fruit growing in the area and the popularity of 'pick your own' fruit farms and this has meant that many freezers in Sussex are filled with berries and currants that can be made into mouth watering desserts throughout the year. Apples too are well utilised, with the expanding development of apple juice and cider production throughout the county.

Honey and Lemon Mousse

Serves 6

3	eggs separated
100g (4 oz)	caster sugar
2	lemons - grated rind and juice
15g (1/2 oz)	gelatine
150ml (5 fl oz)	whipping cream
25 g (1 oz)	Sussex clear honey
	cream and grated chocolate to decorate

1. Whisk together egg yolks, sugar and grated lemon rind.
2. Add 3 tablespoons lemon juice and whisk over a pan of hot water until thick, allow to cool.
3. Dissolve the gelatine in the remaining lemon juice.
4. Fold the whipped cream, whisked egg white, gelatine and honey into the lemon mixture.
5. Leave to set then decorate with whipped cream and grated chocolate.

Mrs S A Steer, Burgess Hill   *See photograph page 23*

Surprising Delight

Serves 6

1/2 kilo (1 1/2 lbs)	cooking apples
100g (4 oz)	sugar
300ml (1/2 pt)	Sussex cider
150g (6 oz)	margarine
150g (6 oz)	caster sugar
3	eggs
150g (6 oz)	self raising flour
150ml (1/4 pt)	fresh whipping cream
50g (2 oz)	grated chocolate

1. Peel, core and slice the apples and stew in a little water, add the sugar and leave them to cool.
2. Add the cider and mix well.
3. Place the margarine, sugar, eggs and flour in a mixing bowl and beat until creamy, adding a little water if necessary.
4. Bake in two 18cm (7 in) sandwich tins for 20-30 minutes at Gas No. 5, 190 degrees C, 375F.
5. Place half of the apple mixture in a serving dish with one of the sandwich cakes on top. Pour over the other half of the apple mixture and place the second cake on top.
6. Whip the cream and spread on the top when the cake is cool.
7. Decorate with grated chocolate.

Jane Cheese, Robertsbridge School

Up, Up and Away!

Sussex is beautiful. From the air - drifting up, up and away in a hot air balloon - it can be spectacular.

"We have taken up dozens of farmers and local landowners as a token of appreciation for allowing the balloon to land on their property", explains Brian Smith who regularly pilots the balloon from his home in Wisborough Green.

The CALA Homes' balloon first appeared in the skies above Sussex in July 1988 when it carried the message 'Better Space for Living' at the first Petworth Park International Balloon Meet.

Since then it has appeared at many other smaller events, giving all sorts of people their first opportunity to travel in a hot air balloon. During its short history, the CALA balloon has gathered many keen fans - the young and the old, the nervous and the brave.

"I know it's not everyone's cup of tea to be suspended in a laundry basket with no visible means of support", says Brian Smith, "but just ask anyone who has tried it. It's beautiful - and they're hooked."

The CALA balloon, over 60 feet high when inflated with 77,000 cubic feet of hot air,

comfortably carries two passengers and the pilot in its willow and cane basket. The balloon flies by heating the air inside the envelope with a flame from two propane-powered burners. Although it can be controlled in flight, by putting more hot air in or taking it out, the direction cannot be controlled - the wind decides which way it will take you.

The balloon regularly raises funds for local charities. "During the past year, we have raised £1,500 for charity. That's about a £1 a mile over the 1,500 miles or so we've travelled", says Brian Smith.

Of course, for CALA Homes, the balloon is a great way to advertise the company and what they build - housing developments like the one, two and three bedroom cottages and apartments at Regent's Place, Pease Pottage and similar new houses are located just off the High Street in Billingshurst with fine views of the Parish Church of St Mary.

On the ground, CALA Homes, and information about the balloon, can be obtained by telephoning (01) 941 1975.

Caffyns - 125 years of a Sussex Family Business

Caffyns had its beginnings in 1865 when William Morris Caffyn, his apprenticeship as ironmonger, tinman and brazier newly completed, opened a small ironmonger's and gas fitter's shop in Meads Road, Eastbourne. In due course, the firm entered the new world of electrical appliances and in 1903 participated in the first Eastbourne Electrical Exhibition held at the Town Hall.

In the same year came the most momentous development of all - the decision to enter the new and exciting world of motoring. In 1906 an ambitious project was completed at Marine Parade. This was a new garage holding 100 cars - much to the astonishment of local residents who were sure that Eastbourne could never have so many!

In 1909 the business became a public company, and two years later the building in Meads Road, so familiar to Eastbourne residents today, was opened next to the site of Williams Morris Caffyn's small shop founded over 40 years earlier.

By 1914 expansion into the rest of Sussex had already begun, with branches at Heathfield and Bexhill. From 1919 onwards a steady programme of development took place throughout Sussex and Kent, with an extension

Caffyn's first garage at the Colonnade, Eastbourne in 1904

of the company's activities into Hampshire, Dorset and Wiltshire in 1977.

Today, the Caffyns Group is still controlled from the Head Office in Meads Road, Eastbourne. Chairman Alan Caffyn, a member of the fourth generation of the Caffyn family, controls a company with a turnover, still increasing, currently about £130 million a year.

Austin Rover cars still form the major part of Caffyns' business. In addition they offer Audi, Mercedes-Benz, Nissan, Renault, Toyota, Vauxhall-Opel, Volkswagen, Land Rover, Range Rover and light commercial vehicles from over 40 branches throughout Sussex, Kent, Hampshire, Dorset and Wiltshire.

Today, Caffyns' facilities include: a computerised locator system for used cars; Flexi-Serve servicing system tailored to individual needs; rapid parts delivery for most makes and contract hire and leasing facilities.

In every town where there is a branch of Caffyns, you open the door to all the resources and expertise of a large professional group, with experience that not only goes back before the motor car even existed, but throughout its trading history has kept right up to date with latest developments, to cater for all your motoring needs.

Caffyn's Austin Rover dealership in Upperton Road, Eastbourne today

Strawberry Profiteroles

Serves 4-6
Choux Paste

150ml (1/4 pt)	water
pinch	salt
50g (2oz)	margarine
100g (4 oz)	plain flour
2	eggs

Mousse

15g (1/2 oz)	gelatine
40g (11/2 oz)	caster sugar
1 tablesp	water
1 tablesp	red wine
1	lemon (juice)
300g (12 oz)	strawberries
150ml (1/4 pt)	double cream (whipped)

1 strawberry jelly dissolved in 120ml (4 fl oz) water
green marzipan and angelica to decorate

Strawberry Profiteroles and, right, Strawberry Cream

Choux Paste
1. Boil water, salt and margarine together.
2. Add flour and beat over the heat to form a ball of smooth mixture.
3. Cool and beat in the eggs.
4. Using a 1cm (1/2 in) nozzle, pipe individual cone shapes about the size of a large cherry.
5. Bake for 15-20 minutes in a hot oven (Gas No. 8, 230 degrees C, 450F).

Strawberry Mousse
1. Dissolve gelatine and sugar in water, cool and add the red wine and lemon juice.
2. Puree the strawberries, add the wine mixture and stir well.
3. Add the whipped cream.
4. When just beginning to set pipe into the profiterole cases.

Completion
1. Dip the profiteroles in the cool strawberry jelly, place in refrigerator to set.
2. Repeat the dipping process 4 or 5 times more until the 'strawberries' are well coated.
3. Top with green marzipan calex and angelica stalk.

This recipe was awarded full marks at the 1988 W.I Ardingly competition and was part of the winning exhibit.

Mrs J McCulloch, Waldron

Strawberry Cream

Serves 8

15g (1/2oz)	powdered gelatine
200g (8 oz)	caster sugar
3	eggs (separated)
1	lemon (grated rind and juice)
400g (1 lb)	strawberries
300ml (1/2 pt)	whipping cream

angelica, strawberries, and cream to decorate

1. Dissolve the gelatine in 150ml (1/4 pt) warm water.
2. Liquidise sugar, egg yolks, lemon rind and juice, strawberries and gelatine.
3. Whip egg whites until stiff.
4. Whip cream, but not too stiff.
5. Fold contents in liquidiser, egg whites and cream together.
6. Place in refrigerator until set.
7. Decorate with angelica, strawberries and cream.

Mrs V C Hoyland, North Heath

Souffle Pancake

Serves 2

Filling

12g (1/2 oz)	butter
1 tablesp	honey
1	eating apple - cubed
1	pear - cubed

Pancake

2	eggs - separated
25g (1 oz)	flour
2 tablesp	milk
1 teasp	caster sugar
pinch	nutmeg or other spice if liked
	butter to fry

1. Melt the butter in a small saucepan, add the honey and fruit, stew gently until tender.
2. Beat together the egg yolks, flour, milk, sugar and spice.
3. Whisk the egg whites until stiff and fold into the yolk mixture.
4. Melt the butter in a frying pan.
5. Pour in the batter and cook gently until the underneath is brown.
6. Cook the top of the pancake under a hot grill.
7. Spread the fruit filling over the top and serve immediately.

A savoury version of this pancake can be prepared by substituting a pinch of salt for the sugar in the batter and preparing a filling of sauted bacon, onion, eating apple and herbs.

Mrs R J Ryan, Hardham

Sussex Pond Pudding

Serves 4-6

200g (8 oz)	flour
1 teasp	baking powder
pinch	salt
100g (4 oz)	shredded suet
100g (4 oz)	currants
	milk to mix
75g (3 oz)	butter
75g (3 oz)	soft brown sugar

1. Mix flour, baking powder, salt, suet and currants.
2. Make into a soft dough with milk.
3. Roll out thickly, leaving sufficient for the lid, and line a pudding basin.
4. Fill the basin with alternate layers of butter and sugar and top with the remaining dough.
5. Cover and steam for two hours.

Mrs Jean Stacy, Hove

200 Years on.....

Lewes Branch of Barclays Bank has been trading as a Bank since July 1789. Founded by a group of traders and landowners, with Viscount Gage its biggest shareholder, Lewes Branch has been serving the agricultural community for two centuries. Some of the Sussex Banks failed to survive the economic 'ups and downs' of the financial world, but whenever there was a crisis of confidence, which happened twice, in the first hundred years of trading, the landowners came to the rescue.

Barclays Bank purchased the Old Bank of Lewes in 1918 and very quickly Barclays grew to a major UK Bank and now the biggest UK International Bank.

Agriculture has always been a major business sector for the Bank, and Barclays employ Agricultural Specialists to ensure that the needs of this sector are met. David Neal-Smith is the Agricultural Manager for the South East based at the Haywards Heath Regional Office. Tony Hume, also a qualified agriculturalist, is a Manager at Lewes Branch which has much farming on its books.

The farming industry is changing and nowhere is this more evident than Sussex. Obviously, efficient agricultural production will continue to

be the main objective for most farmers, but improvements in yields and output have meant that our food requirements can be produced from a smaller area.

At the same time, the rural population has changed with the expansion of the 'commuting belt' and the increase in industry in the South East. The new population considerably more affluent than before is often looking for leisure activities and more 'open space'. This can provide some farmers with opportunities of a non-agricultural nature in meeting these needs.

As time moves on, the agricultural land market in Sussex is noticeably separating into two sectors. The smaller farm in an attractive location with a pleasant residence is often selling to a non-farmer and used for hobby farming or leisure purposes. At the same time, the efficient farmer is looking for good commercial farm land on which to build his business.

Barclays in Sussex is well placed to help and advise both sectors and it is appropriate that Lewes Branch celebrates its Bicentenary in the 1989 'Food and Farming Year', as it looks forward to another 200 years of Agricultural Banking.

50 Years Young

It was in 1921, in the Devon village of Hemyock a few miles south of Taunton, that the children of local milk producers got together to form the first Young Farmers Club in the country, with programmes of calf rearing, competitions and prizes. Ten years later, a national Young Farmers Movement began in earnest. Qualification for joining was the rearing of calves, pigs, poultry and bees and the main purpose of the organisation was agricultural education.

In the 1920s, the Movement came under the umbrella of the Ministry of Agriculture. The Ministry soon realised that help and guidance on the rural side had to come from within the clubs themselves and in 1929 the National Council for Social Service took it over and set out some guidelines. The Movement, it said, existed to give young people under 21 a desire for knowledge of natural things, provide training in stock-raising and public speaking. The clubs should be run by members themselves guided by an adult Leader and committee.

By 1939, there were 412 clubs nationally with a membership of 15,000 and 22 County Federations. Today there are about 50,000 members.

East Sussex YFC began in 1929 with calf, poultry and rabbit keeping classes; it now has 14 clubs and 450 members. West Sussex was formed in 1944 and the County Federation a year later; today it has 10 clubs and 240 members.

Over the years, the structure of YFCs has stayed the same, but there are differences. Mainly, you do not have to come from a farming background to join but just have a love of the countryside and, say the organisers, like having fun. Weekly meetings may include a speaker, a practical demonstration or an outside visit. There are discos and parties, competitions and sports, opportunities to learn agriculture and craft skills, travel abroad, host foreign visitors and care for the surrounding countryside. Clubs raise money for charity, local hospitals, old peoples homes and national emergencies.

Further information can be obtained from the County Organiser, East Sussex County Federation of Young Farmers' Clubs, Plumpton Agricultural College, Plumpton, Lewes, East Sussex BN7 3AE. Tel (0273) 890852; and the County Secretary, West Sussex Federation of Young Farmers' Clubs, YFC Office, West Sussex College of Agriculture and Horticulture, Brinsbury, North Heath, Pulborough, West Sussex RH20 ILD. Tel (07982) 3926.

Summer Fruit Spinning Wheel

Serves 6

Base

150g (6 oz)	muesli
50g (2 oz)	soft brown sugar
75g (3 oz)	margarine - melted

Filling

2	large cooking apples - stewed and sweetened
2	small punnets of raspberries
1 packet	quick jelly mix

1. Add the muesli, and sugar to the melted margarine and press firmly into a shallow 18cm (7 in) dish, refrigerate.
2. Arrange the raspberries on the base in three triangles, pour over the jelly and allow to set.
3. Arrange the apple in between the triangles of raspberries, chill and serve with yoghurt or low fat whipping cream.

If fresh raspberries are not available frozen or canned ones may be used.

Emma Holford, Priory School, Lewes

Gourmet Sweet

Serves 1

125g (5 oz)	Sussex High Weald Dairy sheeps natural thick yoghurt
1 tablesp	runny honey
1 teasp	brandy

Place the yoghurt in a serving dish, pour over the honey and lastly the brandy. Follow with black coffee.

Mrs G St J Hardy, Duddleswell

Sponge Surprise

Serves 6

225g (9 oz)	rhubarb
225g (9 oz)	raspberries
25g (l oz)	sugar
125g (5 oz)	soft margarine
125g (5 oz)	brown sugar
125g (5 oz)	wholemeal self raising flour
2	eggs

1. Wash the rhubarb and cut into 1 cm (1/2") pieces, place in an ovenproof dish with the raspberries and 25g (1 oz) sugar.
2. Place the margarine, sugar, flour and eggs in a mixing bowl and beat until creamy, adding a little water if necessary.
3. Spread the cake mixture over the fruit, bake in a moderate oven (Gas No. 5, 190 degrees C, 375F) for 40 minutes until the sponge is firm.

Susanna Page, Dorothy Stringer School, Brighton

Bartley Mill Muesli Bake

Serves 6

6	thin sliced Muesli bread
40g (1 1/2 oz)	unsalted butter
2 tablesp	raw brown sugar
50g (2 oz)	raspberries
50 g (2 oz)	blackberries
600ml (1 pt)	Sussex double cream
5	eggs
1/2 teasp	cinnamon
1/2 teasp	nutmeg

1. Lightly grease a litre (2 pt) ovenproof dish.
2. Butter the museli bread, cut into quarters, line the base of the dish with the butter side up.
3. Cover bread with a layer of fruit and sugar, repeat, finishing with a layer of bread.
4. Lightly whisk the eggs, cream and spices together.
5. Pour over the pudding and bake in a moderate oven (Gas No. 6, 190 degrees C, 375F) until firm and golden brown.
6. Serve warm.

For a more economical pudding, substitute milk for the cream and add a little more fruit.

Piers Garnham, Frant

Tipsy Sussex Squire

Tipsy Sussex Squire

Serves 5-6

25g (1oz)	ground almonds
6 tablesp	sherry
1 x 18cm (1 x 7 in)	round plain Victoria Sandwich
100g (4 oz)	jam
150ml (1/4 pt)	pouring egg custard
300ml (1/2 pt)	whipping cream
2 tablesp	brandy
25g (1 oz)	flaked almonds (roasted)

1. Mix the ground almonds with half the sherry and spread over the base of a 18 cm (7 in) straight sided serving dish.
2. Split the cake in half and sandwich together with jam, place in the dish and sprinkle with the remaining sherry.
3. Pour the warm custard over the sponge and allow it to soak in, cool.
4. Combine brandy with lightly whipped cream.
5. Cover the whole pudding with cream, decorate with roasted almonds.

This pudding benefits from being made the day before serving to allow the flavours to blend.

Lucy Ann, Alfriston

56

Historic Lewes

It its beautiful Downland setting, the town of Lewes stands out as a signpost to the historic development of our Parliamentary Government. It was here on 14 May 1264, that Simon de Montfort, Earl of Leicester, defeated the army of King Henry III and went on to lay down the principles of democratic government which are now enshrined in the constitutions of similar Parliaments around the world.

The battle headquarters of the Royalists are still standing and may be visited today. The King had installed Prince Edward in Lewes Castle, a Norman fortress built by William de Warrenne who had set up his regional seat of government here after the Battle of Hastings. King Henry himself occupied the Priory of St Pancras, the remains of which still stand in the area of the town known as Southover. The Priory had been established in 1077 and during the following four and a half centuries, until its destruction by Henry VIII, it was the centre of civilisation in medieval Sussex.

It is not surprising that Lewes numbers amongst the top historic towns of England. Everywhere history surrounds us in its buildings, street pattern, and indeed its customs - of which Bonfire Night is a good example. On the night of 5th November the ancient streets of Lewes are thronged with thousands of people clamouring to view the world famous bonfire celebrations organised and presented by the town's numerous bonfire societies. For this one night the street atmosphere in the town is probably unique in its almost medieval flavour.

However, the more usual impression of Lewes is that of an old country market town, as the majority of buildings in its centre belong to centuries long past. A tempting range of shops, olde-worlde pubs and quality restaurants are housed behind Elizabethan and Georgian facades, many of which are mathematical tile patterns. Lewes is not all darkened beams and bow fronts. In the Cliffe, on the east side of the town a new shopping area has been established, where modern stores stand in spacious and attractive surrounds. New industrial estates have been provided on carefully selected sites where facilities and working conditions are ideal. In addition the town is the administrative centre of East Sussex. Here will be found the principal offices of the County, District and Town Councils, together with the headquarters of the East Sussex Fire Service and the Sussex Police Authority.

The cattle and miscellaneous furniture and effects market day is Monday with the flower and vegetable market held on Tuesday mornings. Early closing day for shopping is Wednesday. For visitors to the town, there is a variety of activities and places to see. **Lewes Castle** is a popular attraction for tourists, particularly because of the splendid views it offers on the town and the surrounding countryside.

Anne of Cleves House was one of the properties given by Henry VIII to his fourth wife on their divorce. Today, this attractive timber-framed house contains impressive displays reflecting Sussex life in centuries past.

Lewes Living History Model enables you to relive the town's 1000 year history in 20 minutes of audio-visual excitement. A superb scale model marvellously recreates Lewes as it really was a century ago - both adults and children will be entranced.

Southover Grange Gardens provides a restful retreat in the heart of Lewes. The gardens are famous for their magnificent trees and colourful displays of bedding plants.

Alternatively, a restful stroll can be taken through shady twittens, the Sussex name for narrow lanes between houses.

Augustinian Prior to Tipsy Sussex Squire

The Augustinian Priory founded in 1229 is on an earlier island site and became a Tudor farmhouse in the 16th century. Owned by the Sackville family from 1603 to 1897, the beautiful grounds are enclosed by a medieval moat approached through the imposing 14th century Gate House.

With the resurgence of interest in specifically regional dishes, most areas have become proud of their specialities. Michelham Priory Country Foods very definitely promote the 'Taste of Sussex', serving food produced with fresh ingredients in most cases according to traditional recipes.

Its Sussex Pie, Tipsy Sussex Squire, local Herb Sausages and Sussex Pond Pudding are but a few examples. The bread made in the small Bakery uses flour ground in the Priory Mill.

Visitors to the Priory are able to enjoy not only the very beautiful setting but also a country lunch or Sussex cream tea in the restaurant. In

addition, the 17th century barn is used for private parties both during the day and the evening.

Michelham Country Foods is at Michelham Priory, Upper Dicker, Nr Hailsham, East Sussex. Tel (0323) 440161.

Our Daily Bread

Every day, in the United Kingdom, we eat the equivalent of over 10 million large loaves. According to archaeological research, bread was made and eaten at least 7500 years ago. Later the Hebrews, Greeks and Romans all knew bread as a staple item of diet.

Until 1900, the British baking industry consisted almost exclusively of independent master bakers, who worked largely by hand and sold products from shops attached to their bakeries. The growth of automated plant baking, based upon the development of flowline production (including mechanical slicing and wrapping), occurred as the market widened and motor transport developed.

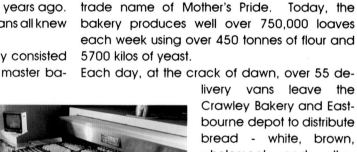

In Sussex, British Bakeries was originally built on a Crawley site in 1958. By the end of the 1960's the bakery operated under the well known trade name of Mother's Pride. Today, the bakery produces well over 750,000 loaves each week using over 450 tonnes of flour and 5700 kilos of yeast.

Each day, at the crack of dawn, over 55 delivery vans leave the Crawley Bakery and Eastbourne depot to distribute bread - white, brown, wholemeal and other morning goods - to most major retail outlets in Sussex and surrounding districts.

Their daily round means your daily bread.

Home Baking, Preserves and Drinks

The trend towards a fibre rich diet has meant that more people are using wholemeal flour. This has been good news for the small mills of Sussex who grind specialist flours that make excellent bread, cakes and biscuits. The apiarists find plenty of sites for their hives and Sussex honey, made mainly from mixed flowers, is recommended by a number of recipe writers.

Singleton Biscuits

Yield 30-40

100g (4 oz)	butter
50g (2 oz)	semolina
100g (4 oz)	wholemeal flour
50g (2 oz)	chopped nuts (any variety)
50g (2 oz)	soft brown sugar
2 tablesp	honey
1	egg (large)
50g (2 oz)	toasted hazelnuts - for decoration
chocolate - melted (optional)	

1. Soften the butter and add the other ingredients including the egg.
2. Mix well (this can be done quickly in a food processor).
3. Divide the dough into 30-40 pieces and roll each in a little flour.
4. Place on bakewell paper on a baking sheet and flatten with a fork.
5. Bake in a moderate oven (Gas No. 4, 180 degrees C, 350F) for 15-20 minutes.
6. Place a half hazelnut on each when the biscuits have softened in the oven.
7. When cool, dribble some melted chocolate over the biscuits at right angles to the fork marks.

Sylvia Jones, East Ashling   *See photograph page 60*

Gypsy Bread

Serves 8

250g (10 oz)	Self raising flour
pinch	salt
pinch	mixed spice
1/2 teasp	ground ginger
100g (4 oz)	soft brown sugar
150g (6oz)	sultanas
50g (2 oz)	chopped peel
150g (6 oz)	treacle
1 tablesp	milk
1	egg
1/2 teasp	bicarbonate of soda

1. Mix together flour, salt, spice, sugar and fruit in bowl.
2. Warm treacle and milk in a pan (do not boil) remove from heat and add egg and whisk well.
3. Dissolve the bicarbonate of soda in a little water and add with the treacle to the dry ingredients in the bowl.
4. Mix well and pour into a greased 1 kilo (2 lb) loaf tin.
5. Bake at Gas No. 4, 180 degrees C, 350F, for 45 minutes then reduce heat to Gas No. 3, 160 degrees C, 325F for a further 30 minutes.

Samantha Petty, Robertsbridge School

Sussex Honey Cake

Serves 12

100g (4 oz)	butter
100g (4 oz)	caster sugar
2	eggs - beaten
100g (4 oz)	Sussex honey
200g (8 oz)	Self raising flour
1 1/2 teasp	mixed spice
	milk if necessary

1. Cream butter and sugar together, add eggs and honey, beat well.
2. Sieve flour and spice together and add to mixture, add milk if mixture seems a little thick.
3. Pour into a greased and lined baking tin 20cm (8 in) square.
4. Bake at Gas No. 6, 200 degrees C, 400F for 20-25 minutes.

Mrs B C Standing, East Preston

Chanctonbury Carrot Cake

200g (8 oz)	soft brown sugar
150ml (6 fl oz)	corn oil
2	eggs
1 1/2 cups	grated carrot
100g (4 oz)	wholemeal flour
1 teasp	baking powder
1/2 teasp	ground ginger
1/2 teasp	grated nutmeg
1	teasp grated orange rind
large pinch	salt
100g (4 oz)	raisins - chopped
50g (2 oz)	walnuts - chopped
Topping - Cream Cheese Frosting	
100g (4 oz)	cream cheese
50g (2 oz)	butter
1 teasp	orange rind
200g (8 oz)	icing sugar - sifted

Chanctonbury Carrot Cake, Sussex Honey Cake and Singleton Biscuits

1. Beat the sugar with the corn oil until well mixed, add the eggs, one at a time, beating well after adding each.
2. Add the grated carrot and mix well.
3. Sift the flour with the baking powder, spices and salt.
4. Place the raisins, walnuts and orange rind in a second bowl, sift the flour mixture over them and toss well to mix.
5. Fold the fruit and flour mixture into the first bowl with the sugar, oil, eggs and carrots. Stir in lightly but thoroughly.
6. Spoon the mixture into a greased and lined 2 lb loaf tin.
7. Bake in a moderate oven (Gas No. 4, 180 degrees C, 350F) for 40-45 minutes.
8. Cool in tin for a few minutes before turning out onto a wire tray.
9. Make the topping by blending the ingredients together thoroughly.
10. Spread over the cake and feather with a fork.

Sue J Coleman, Adversane

Walkers at Pagham Harbour Local Nature Reserve, managed by West Sussex County Council since 1964

Sussex: A Very Special County

For many years, West Sussex County Council's Coast and Countryside Committee has been working to conserve our countryside and to enable people to enjoy it. One consequence of increased leisure time and greater public interest in the countryside and in healthy activities, has been an explosion of interest in country walking.

The County Council maintains the 2500 miles of public paths in the county, makes sure the routes are signposted and liaises with farmers and landowners about obstructions and diversions. Close working relationships have also been developed with ramblers' groups and representatives of other path users.

As a result, and given the attractive countryside of West Sussex, more than half of which is designated as areas of outstanding natural beauty, the county enjoys a public path network second to none in the country.

To assist people to use the paths, the County Council has for the last ten years, organised an annual programme of guided walks from May to October, led by volunteer leaders. In 1988 more than 4000 people took part in the 250 walks on offer. New long distance routes have been created along disused railway lines from Three Bridges to East Grinstead (The Worth Way) and from Guildford to Bramber (The Downs Link) but the most popular route remains The South Downs Way, shortly to be extended to Winchester.

To help people to enjoy the Downs, the County Council provides small car parks and picnic areas. It has established a countryside management project in cooperation with the Countryside Commission, and organises an annual walk of the whole of the South Downs Way, enjoyed regularly by over 200 walkers, together with assorted dogs.

Away from the Downs, the County Council manages Pagham Harbour local nature reserve, recently designated a wetland of international importance, two other nature reserves and a most attractive country park at Buchan Park, Crawley.

For further information, contact the County Secretary, West Sussex County Council, County Hall, Chichester PO19 1RQ. Tel (0243) 777902.

Damson Brandy

Makes 1 1/4 bottles

1 bottle	brandy
450g (1lb)	damsons
450g (1lb)	sugar

1. Divide the brandy into two bottles with necks wide enough for the damsons to pass through.
2. Wash the damsons, prick each with a needle and put 225g (1/2 lb) in each bottle.
3. Using a funnel, pour half the sugar in each bottle.
4. Insert an air-tight stopper, shake well and leave to stand.
5. Invert the bottles each day until all the sugar has dissolved.
6. Leave for three months, strain through a cloth.
7. Store for a further three months before serving.

Miss Francis Carder, Coldwaltham

Elderberry Cordial

2.5L (4 pts)	elderberries
2.5L (4 pts)	water - boiling
25g (1 oz)	powdered - cinnamon
12g (1/2 oz)	allspice
12g (1/2 oz)	ginger - bruised
a few	cloves
1.5k (3 1/2 lbs)	brown sugar
1	slice of toast thickly covered with yeast

1. Wash and pick stalks from elderberries, wash well.
2. Add boiling water, spices and sugar, bring to the boil and boil rapidly for 10 minutes.
3. Place in a clean container and float slice of toast with yeast on surface.
4. Bottle when the fermentation has ceased completely.

Mrs Jean Stacy, Hove

Yoghurt Fruit Drink

Serves 2

25g (1 oz)	strawberries
25g (1 oz)	blackcurrants (or any other soft fruit)
150g (6 oz)	yoghurt
125ml (1/4 pt)	milk
2 teasp	honey

1. Place the ingredients in a food blender and mix until smooth.
2. Pour into two glasses and serve chilled.

Jason Watson, Bognor Regis Community College

Soda Bread

Serves 4

200g (8 oz)	granary, wholemeal or strong white flour
12g (1/2 oz)	baking powder
	milk and water in equal quantities to mix to a soft dough
1 teasp	sesame seeds

1. Mix flour and baking powder in a large mixing bowl.
2. Stir in sufficient milk and water to form a soft yet firm dough.
3. Knead very lightly on a floured surface, shape into a round.
4. Place on a floured baking tray and cut the top into four.
5. Brush with milk and sprinkle with sesame seeds.
6. Bake in a hot oven (Gas No. 7, 220 degrees C, 425F) for 30-40 minutes, when cooked the bread will sound hollow when tapped on the base.

For savoury soda bread add 50g (2 oz) diced cheese and a chopped onion to the flour.

Lucy Ann, Alfriston

Piccalilli

Piccalilli and Soda Bread

Yield 2 kilo (5 lbs)

900g (2 lbs)	green tomatoes
450g (1 lb)	onions - sliced
450g (1 lb)	courgettes - sliced
1	cucumber - diced
1	marrow - diced
1	cauliflower - in florets
100g (4 oz)	salt
Brine Solution	
1.125L (2 pts)	white vinegar
1.25L (2 1/2 pts)	water
25g (1oz)	pickling spice
1 teasp	mustard seed
1 tablesp	turmeric
1 tablesp	mustard powder
1 tablesp	ground ginger
25g (1 oz)	cornflour
200g (8 oz)	demerara sugar

1. Cover prepared vegetables with brine solution and leave overnight.
2. Rinse and drain vegetables.
3. Add spices to 750ml (1 1/4 pts) vinegar, bring to the boil and simmer for 5 minutes, strain and return to the saucepan.
4. Blend the cornflour and sugar with the remaining vinegar, add to the spice solution with the vegetables.
5. Bring to the boil and simmer for 10 minutes.
6. Pour into clean hot jars, cover and seal.

Mrs P Huggins, Littlehampton

Acknowledgements

To the British Food and Farming Publicity Committee for the stamina of its members' long suffering and dedication to the cause.

To the Recipe Competition Sub-Committee for the production of the original Taste of Sussex recipe collection and subsequent detailed preparation for the food photography in this book.

To non-committee members on the Brinsbury College staff who have done so much work behind the scenes.

To Angela Wigglesworth for writing the introductory article about Sussex, to Hilly Hoar for photographing the recipes and to Martin Ash for designing the front cover.

Last but not least to all the subscribers without whom the publication would not have been possible.

Index

Recipes

Starters, Snacks and Suppers

Fish

Poultry, Meat and Game

Puddings and Desserts

Home Baking, Preserves and Drinks

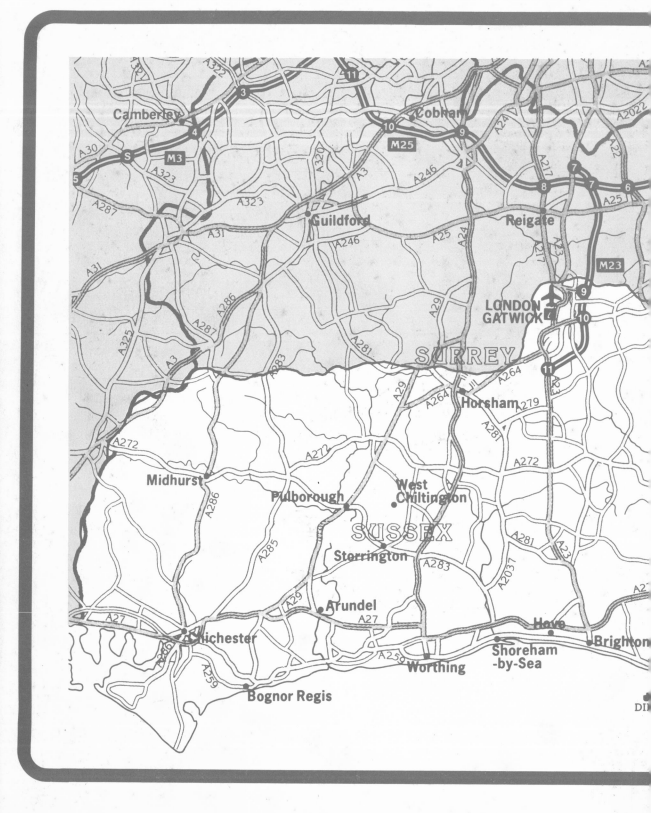